The Life of Saint Columba
As Told by Saint Adomnán

The Life of Saint Columba
As Told by Saint Adomnán

Edited with an Introduction by
Phillip Campbell

CRuachan
Hill Press

ISBN: 978-1-957206-05-9

Cover Art by A.R. Danziger, A. R. Danziger Art & Design
www.ardanziger.com

cRuachan
HiLL PRESS

Published by
Cruachan Hill Press
12552 E Michigan Ave.
Grass Lake, MI 49240
www.cruachanhill.com

Printed and Bound in the United States of America

Dedication and Acknowledgement

This book is dedicated to Amanda Danziger, a true Iona scribe, who not only did the cover artwork but has been a blessed help to me on many projects large and small over the years. This is also dedicated to John Goodall, an honorable Scotsman and love of all the *sancti obscure* of Caledonia. Special thanks to Elizabeth Dawson for her contributions to the introductory essay, to Sarah Grant and Mediatrix Press for copyediting, to Jesse Griffiths for doing the layout, and especially to Maria Russell for her lively interest in this project.

May the prayers of all the saints of Ireland and Scotland
aid the Church of the Holy Isle.

Table of Contents

Introduction
The Genius of Irish Catholicism

by Phillip Campbell

T he Irish are known for many things, such as their generous hospitality, quick wit, and fighting spirit; but most importantly they are known for their resounding faith. From the earliest days of Christendom, the Emerald Isle has been renowned as the land of saints and scholars. For centuries, to be Irish was to be Catholic. The Irish people have a deep devotion to the Holy Family, the Trinity, and the Blessed Mother. Often this faith was defined in the fires of English oppression, giving rise to a Catholicism both hearty and enduring.

The pre-Christian Celts in Ireland were always a deeply religious people, steeped in the folklore of their gods and heroes. Celtic paganism is characterized by its deep sense of the supernatural—of the spiritual realities that lurk behind the created world. For the Celts the veil between the natural and supernatural was thin; the natural was vivified by the spiritual world, which settled like a vapor upon the world of the senses.

The pagan Celts thus had a lively awareness of the importance of the supernatural and the action of the divine upon the created order, even if this sense was blinded by the darkness that necessarily comes with paganism. Even so, perhaps no people since the Greeks had ever been so naturally well-disposed to receive the Gospel of Christ. The reception of the Gospel by the people of Eire will always be tied to the stories of the great Apostle of Ireland, St. Patrick.

Though the Irish had some contact with Christianity prior to the 4th century, it was the mission of St. Patrick that proved the pivotal moment in the Christianization of Ireland. A tradition dating from the 7th century has it that Patrick's mission in Eire was inaugurated on the night of the Paschal Vigil. The Great Vigil of Easter coincided with a significant pagan festival, which required that the fire in every hearth through all of Erin be extinguished on this day until the druids lit the great fire on the Hill of Tara—the seat of High Kings and dwelling place of the gods. If any person dared light a fire on this night he would be subject to the severest of punishments. St. Patrick did not allow the threat of punishment to keep him from celebrating the Paschal Vigil. The saint ascended the Hill of Slane, which can be seen from the Hill of Tara (there is a 9.9-mile distance between them), and lit a tremendous Paschal fire for all to see.

The High King at that time was King Leaghaire. Seeing the flames from the Paschal fire from his court at Tara, Leaghaire asked his council of druids what this portended, since the fire on the Hill of Tara had not yet been lit. The druids warned their king that if the fire were not extinguished that night it would burn in Erin forever.

King Leaghaire summoned St. Patrick to his court to question his blatant defiance of the royal edict. What happened is well known: Patrick faced down the druids in a show of God's divine power. Impressed and certainly frightened, King Leaghaire allowed St. Patrick freedom to roam his kingdom and spread Christianity to all those that were willing to open their hearts to the truth.

St. Patrick travelled all through Erin speaking to anyone who would listen, igniting the love of Christ in the hearts of the Irish people. St. Patrick's Paschal fire did indeed spread throughout the land, growing bigger and brighter with each conversion to the Catholic faith. The druids of King Leaghaire's court had warned their monarch that if the fire on the Hill of Slane was not extinguished it would burn forever. That is precisely what happened.

Irish Catholicism furnishes perhaps the best example of the *enculturation* of the Christian faith. The meaning of enculturation has become somewhat muddled in the period after the Second Vatican Council (1962-1965), wrongly taken by many to mean the syncretic blending of the Christian faith with indigenous paganism. But taken in its proper sense, enculturation is simply another word for Christianization, the process by which the Christian faith works its way into indigenous pagan culture and reorients it towards Christ. What is not compatible with Christian revelation withers and fades; what is compatible becomes formed in the image of the Gospel, purified of its pagan connotations, and ordered to the glorification of God and His Church. Enculturation is thus the manner by which a society properly integrates Christianity into its own native customs, and in turn allowing them to be formed by the Christian faith.

The Irish people embraced the Christian faith with a fiery zeal. Within a century of St. Patrick, the land of Erin was dotted with monasteries from end to end. Kings and nobles embraced Christianity warmly, patronized the Church, and supported the Irish missions. Before long the Irish themselves were sending missionaries abroad to establish Christianity in a Europe torn by the barbarian invasions that came in the wake of the collapse of the Roman Empire. This is known as the golden age of Irish Catholicism, a period lasting roughly from the 5th-8th centuries.

In the 9th century the Irish church suffered a devastating blow from the Viking invasions. Many Irish abbeys were raided or destroyed, including St. Columba's beloved Iona Abbey. Further setbacks were to come when the Normans under Richard Strongbow took advantage of a dispute amongst the Irish nobility to seize control of Ireland in 1170.

Though politically subjugated by first the Vikings and then the Normans, the vitality of the Irish faith continued unabated into the high Middle Ages. While the Normans introduced their own customs of land ownership, architectural style, and of course filled the most important bishoprics with their own people, the Normans and the Irish shared one faith, and the high Middle Ages witnessed a sort of Irish renaissance under an Irish-Norman hybridization.

The trials that would beset Ireland in the early modern period were of an entirely different order. The Protestants under Elizabeth, Cromwell, and the successive rulers of England inflicted horrors upon the Irish Catholics to break their independent spirit and eradicate their ancient faith. The Irish Catholics faced a persecution worse than anything ever perpetrated by the pagan druids. Thousands of Irish were murdered or starved to death as the Church of Éire was glorified by scores of martyrdoms. As of today, twenty-one of these martyrs have been canonized or beatified.

Still, the tenacious attachment of the Irish to the Catholic faith continued and bore them through centuries of domination. When the Irish finally obtained their independence from Great Britain, the Constitution adopted in 1937 began with the following Preamble:

> In the Name of the Most Holy Trinity, from Whom is all authority and to Whom, as our final end, all actions both of men and States must be referred, We, the people of Éire, humbly acknowledging all our obligations to our Divine Lord, Jesus Christ, Who sustained our fathers through centuries of trial, gratefully remembering their heroic and unremitting struggle to regain the rightful independence of our Nation, and

seeking to promote the common good, with due observance of Prudence, Justice and Charity, so that the dignity and freedom of the individual may be assured, true social order attained, the unity of our country restored, and concord established with other nations, do hereby adopt, enact, and give to ourselves this Constitution.

According to a popular tradition, God told St. Patrick that Ireland would never lose the Catholic faith but would sink into the ocean seven years before the Day of Judgment. Indeed, Irish Catholicism has historically demonstrated a pugilistic tenacity that has defied all attempts to expunge it. The particular genius of the Irish Catholic spirit has made Irish Catholicism one of the most potent strains of Christianity in history. Whether considering the missionary zeal of the golden age or the beautiful illuminations of the medieval period, whether the perseverance of the suffering Irish under Protestant persecution or the patient, hard-working disposition of the thousands of Irish priests who became such a familiar staple of 19th and 20th century Catholicism in the English-speaking world, the Christian culture of the Irish people is utterly unique in the history of Christendom.

A great multitude of Irish men and women created this legacy. This book tells the story of just one of these gallant sons of Éire, St. Columba of Iona.

The *Sancti Obscuri* of Ireland

From the beginning of Christianity, the Catholic Church has honored men and women who have demonstrated exceptional holiness in the practice of their faith by designating them *saints*. These saints serve not only as role models for the Christian life, but also as powerful intercessors before the throne of God, where, with and in Christ, they ever live to make intercession for us.

Christian history presents us with an amazing diversity of saints; men and women from every corner of earth, every station in life, every profession: hermits, bishops, monks, nuns, kings, priests, popes, and laity. It is an enduring testament to the holiness of the Church, the Bride of Christ, who, by her unity with Jesus Christ, in every age and place raises up witnesses to His power.

Still, every age has their own favorite saints. If we were to take a survey of Catholic piety in the West of the early 21st century to find out what saints are most popular, we would see St. Therese of Lisieux and St. Padre Pio close to the top of the list, along with more traditional favorites like St. Francis of Assisi, St. Joseph, and St. Patrick.

But just as every age has its own favorites, every age also has its saints who slip through the cracks. Perhaps their lives were not as dramatic; perhaps their path to holiness was walked in relative obscurity. Or perhaps social and political events have effaced their memory, either intentionally or simply through the accidents of time. These sorts of saints are gradually forgotten; their feast days are assigned to others, their shrines fall into neglect, and the details of their lives become shrouded in uncertainty. In some cases, everything about them is lost, even what nation they came from or when they lived. Sometimes they are remembered only from a few place names testifying to the existence of some long forgotten local *cultus*.

These are history's obscure saints, the *sancti obscuri*. Many of the saints of Ireland have unfortunately wound up in this category. During Ireland's golden age, great swaths of Britain and Scotland were evangelized by zealous monks from Éire. These monks, men like St. Columba and his biographer St. Adomnán, founded monasteries and brought the Christian faith to the Britons, Picts, and Gaels of western Britain. It is to these sons of St. Patrick that the earliest establishment of Christianity in Britain owes its foundation.

But beginning in the 7th century, Benedictine monks from the continent brought Christianity to the Anglo-Saxon kingdoms of southern and eastern Britain. The real differences between the Christianity of the Anglo-Saxons and the Irish were negligible, perhaps save their famous debates on the dating of Easter. Nevertheless, disputes were exacerbated by cultural hostility and linguistic differences.. At the Synod of Whitby in 664, it was decided that England should observe the usages of the Anglo-Saxons, and henceforth the Irish customs went into decline in Britain.

That is not to say the work of the Irish saints in the region as forgotten; St. Bede makes mention of many of them in his famous work, the *Historia ecclesiastica gentis Anglorum.* Anglo-Saxon Christianity was very cognizant of the debt it owed to its Irish forebears. But as time went on, it was perhaps inevitable that the early Irish saints would be displaced in popular piety by England's own Anglo-Saxon heroes, such as St. Oswald, St. Dunstan, St. Cuthbert, and so on. Thus, with few exceptions, the Irish saints were confined to veneration within their own island.

Even veneration within Éire was suppressed during the long night of English Protestant domination, which began during the time of Cromwell and continued into the 20th century. The English had been present in Ireland since 1169, but until the Reformation the English and Irish shared a common faith. After the time of Cromwell, the English took positive steps to obliterate or at least suppress Catholicism within Ireland. Though the Irish clung to their precious heritage with what strength they could muster, the veneration of the Irish saints suffered during this period due to the general prohibition of pilgrimages, public festivals in honor of saints, and other notable signs of devotion.

Many shrines fell into obscurity and the cultus of many an Irish holy man went extinct, save for some legends, half-remembered place names, and a few wells or moss-covered stones somehow connected with the saint.

While most English-speaking Catholics are familiar with St. Benedict, few are familiar with St. Enda of the "Holy Isle" of Aran, who established more foundations than Benedict during his life and trained some of the greatest missionaries of the age. Most are familiar with the great medieval University of Paris, where luminaries like St. Albert the Great, St. Thomas Aquinas, and St. Bonaventure did their greatest intellectual work. But few are familiar with the monastic school of Clonard, established by the great St. Finnian, whose followers became so renowned as to be called the "Twelve Apostles of Ireland," and where the beautiful art of Celtic manuscript illumination was perfected.

St. Columba of Iona is undoubtedly among these great Irish saints whose name deserves to be better known. A disciple of both St. Finnian of Movilla and St. Finnian of Clonard, St. Columba is among one of the "Twelve Apostles of Ireland." His life is as rife with miracles as St. Benedict; his missionary work was incredibly extensive, encompassing northern Ireland, western Scotland, the Hebrides islands, and parts of northwestern England. He is remembered as the Apostle of Scotland for his incredible work among the pagan Picts. His chief monastic foundation at Iona was the most important monastery in Scotland for centuries. He is certainly one of the most important saints ever to come out of Ireland. Yet time and again this author has seen Catholics—many of them devout, life-long practitioners of their faith—go blank when St. Columba is mentioned. For many, the great Columba is another one of the *sancti obscuri*.

Let us now begin to rectify this.

Life and Education of Saint Columba in Ireland

St. Columba was born in 521 in Gartan, now in County Donegal in North Ireland. His parents, Fedlimid and Eithne, were members of the local ruling dynasty, the Uí Néill clan. The Uí Néill were descended from the Niall of the Nine Hostages, High King of Tara who died sometime around 405. Following the death of Niall, the Uí Néill family dominated Leister and Ulster, ruling as petty kings over a small but vibrant northern Irish kingdom.

St. Columba was the great-great-grandson of Niall of the Nine Hostages. He was baptized "Colum", which means "dove", and is sometimes known as Columcille, meaning "Colum of the Churches." Columba lived during the golden age of Irish Catholicism, when the young Christian faith was aggressively shaping the minds and culture of the Irish. Ireland of Columba's day was rife with saints; to this day one cannot go from one village to the next without stumbling across a well, stone, chapel, or shrine associated with some saint from this era.

From St. Columba's earliest years, he had the good fortune to be surrounded by some of these saints. We do not know when or how he discerned his vocation, but it must have been early. It was not uncommon for the children of the nobility to be given to tutors for their education; Columba was tutored as a boy by the priest St. Crunathan (also called Cruithnechán), who seems to have been an uncle of some sort. He taught the young saint to read by reciting the Psalms; according to Adomnán, Crunathan once saw a ball of light hovering over the boy's head as he slept, which portended great things for Columba's future.[1]

Columba is also said to have spent some time with a bard called Gemman in the region of Leinster. This would not have been uncommon in early medieval Ireland, as the bards were the keepers of a family's oral histories and St. Columba would have learned the history of his people—as well as how to speak and sing—from such men. Indeed, Columba must have been well trained in this art, for Adomnán mentions he had a particularly lovely voice.[2] In the company of Gemman he once witnessed the murder of a young girl. This moved him deeply, and in righteous indignation Columba declared that the girl's soul was among the blessed while the murderer would go to hell. The murderer in fact died unrepentant almost immediately, another strange portent which established Columba as a prophet. [3]

As a young man Columba attended the famous monastic school at Movilla, then under the guidance of the celebrated St. Finnian, also known as St. Findbarr. Here young Columba drank deeply from the wellspring of the Irish monastic heritage, then in its hey-day. Irish monasticism of Columba's time was pre-Benedictine. St. Columba himself was a contemporary of St. Benedict, who died when Columba was just beginning his monastic career. Benedictine monasticism would not come to the British Isles until 597 (the year of Columba's death) with the arrival of St. Augustine on Thanet and the beginning of the English missions. What sort of monasticism, then, did Columba imbibe at the monastic school of St. Finnian?

We do not know too much about the particulars of early 6th century Irish monasticism. It is mainly known through archaeological remains and hagiographies, such as the *Vita Columbae*. The early 7th century *Rule of St. Columbanus* probably resembles the rule of life Columba would have known. St. Columbanus's rule is brief, only ten chapters. It emphasizes private confession of faults followed by corporal discipline, strict manual labor, and admonitions to poverty, chastity, and obedience. The most interesting aspect of the *Rule of St. Columbanus* is its provision for perpetual prayer, *laus perennis*. Whereas the *Rule of St. Benedict* punctuates the day with eight canonical hours in which all the monks gather, the *laus perennis* of St. Columbanus has the monks divided into different 'shifts' who relieve each other in the choir throughout the day. The goal of *laus perennis* is that the praises of God be sung in the chapel without ceasing.

St. Columbanus died in 615, eighteen years after St. Columba. His rule reflects the usages at Bangor Abbey in northern Ireland. How much it had in common with what St. Columba would have learned as a boy in Movilla is uncertain, although it is probable that at the *Rule of St. Columbanus* at least preserves the monastic spirit of the preceding century, even the particulars are different from what St. Finnian taught St. Columba.

It was at Movilla that Columba was elevated to the diaconate and where he performed his first miracle. Adomnán tells us that "on a certain feast day St. Finnian found that he was lacking wine for the sacred mysteries. Hearing the ministers of the altar complaining among themselves of this want, he took the vessel and went to the fountain, that, as a deacon, he might bring pure spring water for the celebration of the Holy Eucharist; for at that time he was himself serving in the order of deacon. The holy man then blessed in faith that element of water taken from the spring, invoking, as he did so, the name of our Lord Jesus Christ, who in Cana of Galilee had changed water into wine: and the result was that by His operation in this miracle also, an inferior element, namely pure water, was changed into one of a more excellent kind, namely wine, by the hands of this illustrious man. The holy man, then returning from the fountain and entering the church, placed beside the altar the vessel containing this liquid, and said to the ministers: 'Here is wine, which the Lord Jesus hath sent, for the celebration of His mysteries.' The holy bishop and his ministers having ascertained the fact, returned most ardent thanks to God."[4]

At some point Columba moved on to also study with St. Finnian of Clonard, the other of Ireland's famous Finnians. There exists an apocryphal legend that St. Finnian of Clonard intended Columba to receive episcopal consecration but gave him priestly ordination by mistake. In any case, Columba was apparently ordained to the priesthood around this time by Bishop Etchen of Clonfad.

Columba's movement from Movilla to Clonard, as well as his tutelage under Gemman, seem to indicate that early Irish monasticism lacked the practice of stability—the obligation of the professed monk to remain in the particular monastery in which he was professed unless transferred by a superior, a discipline promoted by the Benedictines. This is only a conjecture; we do not know the details of St. Columba's wanderings. It could very well have been that his superiors recognized his natural abilities and sent him abroad for further training. This is not the image we get of his early years, however. Columba seems to have been rather like an itinerant disciple spending time with this and that mentor, drinking wisdom from various fountains and then moving on as he willed. This is not inconsistent with what we know of early Irish monasticism, which seemed to bring the hermit, missionary, and monk coalescing together into a single profession. There was always a strong eremitic strain in Irish monasticism; Adomnán frequently references wandering hermit-monks who settled on precarious, isolated little rocks dotted throughout the Irish Sea, which the Irish monks affectionately called "deserts in the ocean" (calling to mind the Desert Fathers).[5] This eremitic strain was not uncommon of pre-Benedictine monasticism as a whole: recall the various wandering or abbot-less monks and hermits we encounter in Pope St. Gregory's *Life of St. Benedict.* But it seemed to have been particularly pronounced in the monastic observance of Columba's Ireland.

A pestilence in 544 prompted Columba to strike out on his own, returning to his home around Ulster. In this region he founded several monastic foundations, most notably those of Derry in 548—where several of the miracles related by Adomnán take place—as well as Durrow, and another in Kells. The abbey at

Durrow in County Offaly became famous for its illuminated manuscripts. Columba himself seems to have been a skilled illuminist; Adomnán's *Vita* mentions books written by the saint that had miraculous properties.[6] Another humorous tale relates St. Columba's palpable irritation at having a clumsy monk spill his inkhorn, a man Columba testily describes as "not of very sharp wit."[7] When Columba was in the throes of death, the last thing he did before retiring to his chamber was visit the Scriptorium to transcribe the Psalm 33.[8] A keen interest in manuscripts and their illuminations is one of the few personal traits of Columba that shines through Adomnán's work.

It was his interest in illuminated manuscripts that gave rise to the most famous incident in St. Columba's life, the Battle of Cúl Dreimhne. Sometime around 561, St. Columba returned to Movilla to pay a visit to his old mentor, St. Finnian. Movilla was home to the famous Psalter of St. Finnian, a psalter famed throughout Ireland for its exceptional illuminations. St. Finnian guarded his famous psalter carefully and had forbidden anyone to make copies of it. St. Columba, however, had a taste for beautiful illustrations and began making a copy of the psalter in secret. He was far along copying the book when St. Finnian discovered it and demanded that Columba hand over the copy.

It must be understood that the psalter itself was not the issue. Every monastery of the age would have had a psalter; the psalms were not anybody's private property. Rather, it was the splendid, illuminated illustrations that were at the heart of the contention. Columba wished his own monastery to possess a book as beautifully illustrated as the Psalter of St. Finnian and risked the trust of his old mentor to do so.

Columba refused to hand over the copied psalter. The two men could not come to an agreement on who owned the copy, and thus the matter was brought to the attention of King Diarmait mac Cerbaill, High King of Tara. Diarmait ruled in favor of St. Finnian, famously saying, "To every cow its calf, and to every book its copy," a pun referencing the production vellum parchment from calf skin. Still obstinate, St. Columba fled to his kinsmen, the northern Uí Néill, who shielded Columba from the king's command and took to arms to protect him. This mobilization led to a wholescale rebellion against Diarmait by the Uí Néill. According to the legend, Finnian prayed for the success of King Diarmait's soldiers while Columba prayed for the Uí Néill. In the subsequent battle, Diarmait was defeated by the Uí Néill and 3,000 men were killed.

What happened next is a matter of conjecture. It is certain that St. Columba was genuinely horrified at the slaughter. St. Finnian held him personally responsible for the 3,000 deaths. According to one tradition, Columba sought the advice of his confessor, St. Molaise of Arran, who proscribed a severe penance: leave Ireland to preach the Gospel elsewhere, winning as many souls to Christ as were lost at the Battle of Cúl Dreimhne and never look upon his homeland again. Another Columba legend says that later in life, when summoned back to Ireland to participate in a synod, St. Columba returned wearing a blindfold in order to be faithful to his vow never to look upon Ireland again.

This version of the tale has been looked on with skepticism by some, as it is not mentioned at all in Adomnán's biography. Adomnán may have referenced the Battle of Cúl Dreimhne in passing, however, when he noted that Columba was excommunicated by a synod in Ireland for "very trifling reasons" in some matter which Columba held himself innocent and was vindicated by God.[9] Adomnán never mentions what the "very trifling reasons" for the excommunication were. As a successor abbot at Iona, it is obvious that St. Adomnán did not wish to dwell on the more controversial aspects of Columba's life. This passage certainly may be a reference to the affairs of Cúl Dreimhne. If so, it would suggest that Columba's exile from Ireland was not self-imposed but the result of an excommunication. This offers an interesting alternative to the legendary account.

Historians debate the merits of the various traditions. Some, while acknowledging the Battle of Cúl Dreimhne and Columba's role as an instigator of the Uí Néill, deny the entire story of the Psalter of St. Finnian and focus instead on another episode involving Columba and Diarmait. St. Columba gave shelter in his monastery to a relative, Curnán, son of Áed mac Echach, who had killed a relative of King Diarmait. King Diarmait dragged Curnán out of the monastery and slew him, thus violating the right of sanctuary offered by Columba. In anger, Columba roused the northern Uí Néill and the Battle of Cúl Dreimhne followed. This episode is found in many of the earlier annals, which is why it is favored by those who doubt the story of the psalter.

It is, of course, possible that both accounts are true. The slaying of Curnán occurred in 559. This would have undoubtedly left St. Columba with a poor opinion of King Diarmait, and Diarmait likewise suspicious of Columba as one who offered sanctuary to royal opponents. Though the date of the Battle of Cúl Dreimhne is debated, tradition puts it in 561, three years after the killing of Curnán. When King Diarmait found himself called upon to pass judgment on the Psalter, he ruled in favor of Finnian as a jab of vengeance against Columba for sheltering the king's enemy. St. Columba, twice offended by Diarmait, probably had legitimate doubts about the impartiality of the king's judgment, perhaps seeing his ruling as an exercise of retaliation rather than of justice. He then fled to the Uí Néill, who had been trying to consolidate their own power in the north for some time. These two offenses against their famous kinsman provided the right pretext for rebellion against King Diarmait. And thus the two armies marched off towards Cúl Dreimhne.

And what of Columba's punishment for his part in the battle? Columba certainly may have been excommunicated for his part in riling up the Uí Néill, as Adomnán suggests, but he may have also been encouraged by his confessor St. Molaise to undertake this exile willingly as an act of penance.

As we can see, it is not impossible to reconcile the divergent narratives. It is fascinating to speculate upon, although speculation it must remain. All we know for certain is that, motivated by a desire to save souls, St. Columba and twelve companions crossed the sea to Scotland in a currach (a small, wickerwork boat covered in hide) and landed on the Scottish island of Iona on May 12, 563.

Saint Columba in Exile

Iona is a small island, just shy of 3.5 square miles in area. It is located in the Mull island chain in the Ross of Mull on the western coast of Scotland. The Mull islands themselves are part of a larger group known as the Inner Hebrides, a multitude of rugged islands that border Scotland on the west. Iona sits about 2 miles out from the larger Isle of Mull going west. Exposed to the sea from the west, Iona is swept by powerful ocean breezes and today is devoid of trees; this was probably true in St. Columba's time as well. It is plentiful in rocks, however, and these were used to construct an Iron Age fort on Dùn Ì, a looming 331-foot hill that is Iona's highest point. According to tradition, St. Columba's currach landed near the island's western bay, the Bay at the Back of the Ocean, at a place called Càrn Cùl ri Éirinn, literally "the Hill of Turning Back to Ireland."

At the time Columba landed in Iona, the region was part of the kingdom of Dál Riata, which was then in its ascendancy. Dál Riata was a domain consisting of the Scottish Hebridean islands, along with portions of Ulster in north Ireland and Argyll in western Scotland. At some time in the 4th or 5th century, the peoples of Dál Riata had begun migrating from northern and eastern Ireland into the Scottish Hebrides and eventually to the Scottish mainland around Argyll. Though nominally united under a king ruling from Argyll or Bute in Scotland (at the time of Columba's landing this was Gabrán mac Domangairt) in reality the Dál Riata were separated into several powerful clans with bases in Islay, Kintyre, Mull, and Bute. Contemporary historians refer to them as the Gaels, but in Adomnán's *Vita Columbae* they are the *Scoti*. The homeland of the Dál Riata in Ireland is called "Scotia," and their language is Scotic.

Iona, however, was apparently uninhabited at the time, and St. Columba founded the famous Abbey of Iona on the island shortly after his arrival. Sadly, little remains of the beloved abbey of Columba and Adomnán (the current structure dates from the Norman period). St. Columba quickly won the esteem of the Dál Riatic King Aedán mac Gabráin, son of Gabrán mac Domangairt. King Aedán reigned from 574-609, outliving Columba by twelve years. He appears frequently in Adomnán's work as a supporter of Columba and the object of some of Columba's prophecies. Columba offers heartfelt prayers for the king in his battle with Picts; he lovingly kisses the son of King Aedán and offers prophecies on the fates of his children.[10] Later we see Columba receiving an angelic message that God Himself has established Aedán in the kingship and that Aedán's house will have victory over all its foes.[11]

The Dál Riata (or at least the most eminent among them) seem to have already been Christian by the time of St. Columba's mission to Scotland. The real object of St. Columba's missionary activity would have been the Picts, a pagan tribe that was spread throughout the Scottish Lowlands and parts of Northumbria in England. The Picts were scattered under a series of petty kingdoms ruled by warrior-kings. Like the Irish, their culture was stratified into castes, with a class of druids at the top. As in the old tales of St. Patrick, Columba comes into conflict with the Pictish kings and their Druids and must win their respect by performing miraculous signs. The central Pictish character of Adomnán's *Vita* is "King Brude", known to history as King Bridei (r. 554-584). It is at the fortress of King Brude that Columba will work one of his most famous miracles: St. Columba, his reputation as a miracle worker preceding him, approached the fortress of King Brude to announce to him the Gospel. The king, haughtily dismissive, ordered the solid wooden doors of the fortress shut tightly against Columba. When the holy man approached and found no one willing to open the doors for him, he marked the doors with the sign of the cross in a dramatic gesture. The doors instantly flew open of their own accord, granting Columba access to the stunned king.[12] In another passage, Columba caused a stone to float in the presence of Brude and his entire household.[13]

The druids also deal with Columba's tenacity as the holy man worked miracles at their expense. The *Vita* has a tale in which the druid Broichan (like his counterparts in the life of St. Patrick), enters a contest with the saint and loses. But the relationship between the druids and Columba appears to be one of warm rivalry rather than violent hostility. In one chapter we see Columba demonstrating the might of the Christian God against the druids with a powerful manifestation of divine power, while in the next we see Columba chatting with the very same druid Broichan pleasantly over the details of one of his voyages.[14] Over a century and a half had passed since St. Patrick first brought Christianity to the Celtic peoples. The fiery opposition of the druids who encountered Patrick on the Hill of Slane has in the *Vita Columbae* yielded place to a graceful withdrawal in the face of an inevitable Christianization.

One thing that must strike us is St. Columba's age when he began his mission on Iona. He could not have been any younger than 42 or 43, already well past midlife for a man of the 6th century. In many of Adomnán's stories of Columba at Iona, we get the impression we are dealing with a man already advanced in years. The rustic life of 6th century Ireland and Scotland was harsh on its own; when we reflect that St. Columba and his companions probably practiced mortifications over and above the regular rigors of life, we should be rightly amazed. And when we contemplate that this man, who was already in the sunset of his life when he came to Iona, was not content to stay shut up in his monastery but used Iona as a hopping off point for numerous missionary journeys to the mainland, our amazement should give way to awe at the power of the grace of God.

It is a shame that Adomnán did not devote more space to the missionary journeys of Columba. He narrates some of Columba's more exceptional missionary exploits (such as the miraculous opening of the doors of Brude's fortress) but leaves us no details about the chronology or routes of St. Columba's travels, his manner of evangelizing, or the churches he undoubtedly founded. We catch word of him here and there: we see him in Druim Cett in Ireland in the retinue of King Aedán for a council of kings, and also in Loch Ness where he has history's first recorded encounter with the Loch Ness monster. There are all sorts of locations given from all over Ireland and Scotland, but no real sequence to the narrative. It is only with great difficulty that one can reconstruct any sort of chronology from the *Vita Columbae*, and this only in passing references to certain kings and bishops that help date a certain event. Even then anything like a timeline is merely speculative. All we can piece together is that Columba spent the better part of his life—34 years—laboring among the Picts to win souls for Christ.

After over three decades of apostolic labor among the Picts and the people of Dál Riata, Columba passed away at Iona in his seventy-sixth year. Adomnán tells us that he died shortly after midnight on June 9, 597 near the altar at Iona Abbey, surrounded by his brethren to whom he managed to bless one last time before collapsing.[15] By the time of his death many of the Pictish tribes had embraced Christianity, Iona was renowned as the spiritual center of Scottish-Gaelic Christianity, and monastic houses that looked to Iona were sprouting up all over southwestern Scotland. Columba's beloved kingdom of Dál Riata went into decline a generation after Columba's death, "and from that day to this they have been trodden down by strangers, a fate which pierces the heart with signs and grief" laments Adomnán.[16]

But Iona itself would flourish. Shortly before his death, St. Columba said of Iona, "Small and mean though this place is, yet it shall be held in great and unusual honor, not only by Scotic kings and people, but also by the rulers of foreign and barbarous nations, and by their subjects; the saints also even of other churches shall regard it with no common reverence."[17] These things would all come to pass: Iona would go on to become a kind of royal necropolis for the future Kings of Scotland, whose bodies would be ferried over to Iona to be interred amidst the singing and prayers of the Iona monks. The words to this beautiful "Boat Song of Iona" are included in the Appendix.

The golden age of Iona unfortunately came to an end in 825 when the Vikings devastated the monastery and slaughtered its monks. Still, the legacy of Columba and his monks lives on in the little green island straddling the Ross of Mull, its bay where Columba landed in the summer of 563 still gazing westward across the emerald blue waters of the Irish Sea to the land of Éire, the homeland of so many saints.

Saint Adomnán of Iona

We cannot complete our sketch of St. Columba's life without mentioning the man with whom his name is forever entwined, his successor St. Adomnán. Just as St. Benedict was made known through the writing of Pope St. Gregory and St. Francis through the biography of St. Bonaventure, so we know of St. Columba primarily through the writings of St. Adomnán.[18]

Adomnán (624-704) succeeded St. Columba to the abbacy of Iona in 679, the ninth in line after the saint. Adomnán lived at a time when it was still possible to tap into the living memory of St. Columba, but when that memory was fading rapidly. Adomnán himself was too young to have ever known Columba, being born twenty-seven years after St. Columba's passing. But there were still old monks living in Adomnán's day who were recipients of Columba's miracles or who had witnessed his prophecies come to pass. And Adomnán himself had experienced the power of St. Columba's intercession firsthand. He relates:

> ...our monastery was requiring repairs, and some oak-trees were to be taken from near the mouth of the river Sale (the Seil, in Lorn), in twelve vessels which we brought for the purpose. Our sailors then rowed out to sea with their oars, the day being calm and the sea tranquil, when suddenly a westerly wind, which is also called Zephyr, sprang up, and we betook ourselves to the nearest island, which is called in Scotic Airthrago, to seek for shelter in a harbor in it.
>
> But in the meantime, we began to complain of this unfavorable change in the wind, and in some measure even to blame our Columba, saying, "Doth our unfortunate detention in this place please thee, O saint? Hitherto we had hoped that we might receive from thee some aid and comfort in our labors through the divine favor, seeing we thought that thou wert honored and powerful in the sight of God.

No sooner had we thus spoken, than, wonderful to relate, the unfavorable west wind ceased, and immediately, in the course as it were of one minute, behold a most favorable south-eastern breeze sprang up. The sailors were then directed to raise the sail yards in the form of a cross, and spread the sails upon them; thus putting to sea with a steady and favorable breeze, we were enabled, without the slightest fatigue, to reach our island that same day, rejoicing in our cargo of wood, and in the company of all who were engaged in assisting us in the ships. Thus, the chiding with the holy man, slight though it was, in that complaint assisted us not a little; and in what and how great esteem the saint is held by the Lord is evident from His hearing him so quickly and changing the winds.[19]

Adomnán goes on to say that he witnessed such miracles not once but three times personally.

What we know of St. Adomnán comes from St. Bede's *Historia ecclesiastica gentis Anglorum.* St. Bede calls him "a wise and worthy man, excellently grounded in the knowledge of the Scriptures." He describes how St. Adomnán pleaded with his monastic following at Iona, which was "very small and situated in a remote corner of the world," to accept the customs of the continental Church rather than those peculiar to Ireland.[20]

The most important of these customs would have been the date of the celebration of Easter, something contested between the Irish and the English churches. Though in theory the Irish had agreed to adopt the Roman dating at the Synod of Whitby in 664, the monks of Iona and its daughter houses persisted in the old Irish method of calculating Easter for some time after. Though sincere in his opinion, St. Adomnán ultimately failed to win the

Ionan monks over and eventually left Iona for missionary work in Ireland before returning to die in Iona in 704.

St. Adomnán was a gifted author, writing not only the *Vita Columbae* but also a book on the Holy Land, which he presented as a gift to King Aldfrith of Northumbria. He also wrote a fair amount of Gaelic verse.

Saint Columba and Hagiography

So much for the life and times of Columba and Adomnán. But what of St. Columba the man. What sort of person was he? What kind of character emerges from behind the writing of Adomnán?

Contemporary historians have tended to dislike hagiography. Part of this is an implicit anti-supernatural bias against the miracle stories related in the medieval *Vitae*. For the modern secular historian, miracle stories, such as those related of Columba by Adomnán, are of no historical value except inasmuch as they tell us what the Irish Christians of Adomnán's time *believed* about St. Columba. No credence is given to them as objective historical facts of Columba's life.

But more central to the modern distaste for the genre is that the hagiographies of the Middle Ages tend to focus on what was exceptional or out of the ordinary about their subject. The hagiographer is not merely presenting a chronological biography, but rather a confession of the mighty works of God wrought through the saint. The hagiography does not dwell on what is common to all men but what is unique to the saint. Its purpose is to demonstrate why their subjects should be considered saintly.

The secular historian is irritated by this, as such an approach tells us very little about what constituted the saint's ordinary existence. In Adomnán's work we find no details of how St. Columba spent his average day, no chronological record of his travels, no glimpses into the inner workings of the Iona community. Instead, we find detailed narratives of the saint's miracles, prophecies, and visions.

The secular historian reasons from this to the conclusion that the *Vita Columbae* is unreliable as history. But the historical value of hagiography should not be so quickly written off. It is not that the medieval hagiographer disregards the facts, only that he is not concerned with the same set of facts as the modern historian. The facts the hagiographer chooses to relate are those which he finds most essential to understanding the subject, but this is no grounds for objection. It is simply what different historiographical genres do. We might similarly object to a Freudian history dwelling on personal and family relationships, or a military historian's emphasis on battles, or a Marxist historian narrowing in on economic and power struggles. But while the Freudian, military, and Marxist schools have all been accepted into the historiographical canon by the moderns, the hagiographer is regrettably omitted.

This reveals the real bias of the modern secular historian against hagiography: it is not that the hagiographer chooses to focus on one aspect of history (many historiographical schools do this); rather, it is the particular aspect of history that the hagiographer deals in—the miraculous—that so offends the modern historian, for anti-supernaturalism is taken as an *a priori* assumption.

It is not within the scope of this essay to provide an apologetic for accepting supernatural claims in historical works, except to note that rejection of the supernatural is always based on philosophical *a priori* assumptions, not scientific or historical facts. It is certainly scientific to argue that this or that miracle may or may not have happened based on the evidence in that particular case, but it is not scientific to argue that there can never be supernatural activity whatsoever. To make this assumption is to leap from science into philosophical presuppositions about the universe.

Thus, people of faith must come to a work like the *Vita Columbae* with a different mindset. Saints are not two-dimensional figures who simply emerge without any sort of backstory or great deeds. If St. Columba did not do any of the miraculous works Adomnán attributes to him, we may justly wonder why he was so venerated. The modern skeptic assumes that the legendary elements of the *Vita* were written back after the fact to bolster the status of the already legendary saint. The person of faith understands that the opposite is in fact the case: the saint has achieved legendary status *because* of his great and often miraculous works. If he had not performed these works, he would not have enjoyed the cultus of which the *Vita* was a product.

Thus, while moderns see the *Vita* obscuring the person of the saint, for the Catholic, the *Vita* throws the saint into relief. We are able to discern the real personality of the saint through the *Vita*. The modern error is unfortunate, for those who denigrate the testimonies of the *Vita* in search for an elusive "historical saint" are doomed to fail, just like those Scripture scholars who dismiss the "Christ of faith" in a futile search for the "Jesus of history." Of course, the Jesus of history and the Christ of faith are one and the same—and the St. Columba of the hagiography and the historical Columba are identical.

As mentioned above, though Adomnán was not born until twenty-seven years after Columba's death, there were still many around in his day who had encountered Columba in their youth or who had known persons who had witnessed Columba's miracles. Granted, details of certain stories could have been confused: two different accounts could be merged into one, or a single story, through variations in retelling, becomes multiplied. But this does not mean Adomnán's work is unreliable in the whole. He goes to great pains to verify his sources, stating "from whose lips I myself have come to know all that I have stated" so we know he is relating information firsthand. In another place he relates a miracle, assuring us "and this I myself was told." He says of one miracle that "there are yet living, not merely one or two witnesses as the law requires, but hundreds and more who can bear testimony."[21] He informs us that he learned of a certain prophecy of Columba second-hand, "for Lugbe himself, after St. Columba's death, bore witness in the presence of other holy men, from whom I learned the undoubted truths which I have now related of the saint."[22] In relating one vision he tells us "Comman, sister's son to Virgnous, a respected priest, solemnly assured me, Adomnán, of the truth of the vision I have just described, and he added, moreover, that he heard the story from the lips of the abbot Virgnous, his own uncle, who, as far as he could, had seen that vision."[23] Adomnán is solicitous to identify his sources when he can and ensures us that he presents their testimonies just as he heard them.

And what can we learn about the person of Columba from Adomnán's work? Adomnán divides his *Vita* into three sections, dealing with St. Columba's prophetic gifts, his miraculous powers, and his encounters with the holy angels. Within each book the stories are grouped topically, not chronologically. For example, two prophecies or healings that share certain characteristics may be grouped side by side in the text even though occurring decades apart. Adomnán frequently jumps around between Columba's life in Ireland, his years on Iona, and his missionary travels. Events from his youth and old age are juxtaposed with priority going to the subject matter, not the chronology.

The picture of St. Columba that emerges from these diverse tales is of a fiery prophet, a man who beholds God directly and sees the whole world in Him. Book One in the *Vita* is devoted to St. Columba's prophetic revelations. The prophetic anecdotes all take a similar form: at such-and-such a time, St. Columba told so-and-so that such would come to pass, and so it did. Occasionally we learn a little more; in Book One, we see the veil momentarily pulled back, as Lugbe, one of Columba's disciples, asks Columba how these prophecies come to him, "whether by sight, or hearing, or other means unknown to man." St. Columba's answer is probably the most fascinating passage of his *Vita* and gives us the greatest insight into his character as a prophet:

> To this the saint replied, "Thy question regards a most difficult subject, on which I can give thee no information whatsoever, unless thou first strictly promise, on thy bended knees, by the name of the Most High God, never to communicate this secret mystery to any person all the days of my life." Hearing this Lugbe fell at once on his knees, and, with face bent down to the ground, promised everything faithfully as the saint demanded.
>
> After this pledge had been promptly given he arose, and the saint said to him, "There are some, though very few, who are enabled by divine grace to see most clearly and distinctly the whole compass of the world, and to embrace within their own wondrously enlarged mental capacity the utmost limits of the heavens and the earth at the same moment, as if all were illumined by a single ray of the sun."[24]

Though Columba had the fire of a prophet, he was not a tormented soul. Some saints are like Jacob, wrestling with God in the anguish of a soul perpetually in turmoil. We might imagine St. Teresa of Avila struggling with God through her periods of dryness, or St. Francis of Assisi making a wife and children for himself out of snow before smashing them in a fit of frenzied renunciation.[25] We could cite of the ecstatic praise and worship of St. Philip Neri or the suffering spirituality of St. Catherine of Siena. Columba's holiness is a world away from these sorts of passionate saints. St. Columba's holiness is permeated with patience and certitude grounded in God's omnipotence. St. Columba does not wrestle with scruples or break into spontaneous hymns of praise; he neither gets carried away in transports of divine ecstasy nor struggles through dark nights. Rather, from his seat in Iona he calmly sees the plans of God unfolding upon the broad plain of the world the way a man gazes upon the breadth of the sea. "He knew with the eyes of his soul what he could not see taking place...with the eyes of his body," St. Adomnán wrote.[26] Columba's eye sees the world, but through God. Or, in the saint's own words, he beholds "the utmost limits of the heavens and the earth at the same moment, as if all were illumined by a single ray of the sun." St. Columba is seated in heavenly places. He is not perturbed by the movements of his soul or the things he encounters in the world. God's will governs everything, from the rise and fall of kings down to the inkhorn spilled in the saint's lap by a clumsy monk. All one can do is marvel at God's amazing providence, trust in His governance, and through His grace, keep oneself unspotted from the wickedness of the world. Columba's holiness is one of imperturbable tranquility. This is the Columba's spirituality as presented to us by Adomnán.

St. Columba is not the only character that emerges in the *Vita*. We have already mentioned King Aedán, St. Finnian, the druid Broichan, the Pictish King Brude, and even Adomnán himself, all of whom recur in the *Vita*. We should also mention some of St. Columba's disciples who give depth to Adomnán's portrait by revealing how the saint interacted with his monks, thus lifting the veil to show us what life was like at Iona. Like Brother Leo and Brother Masseo in the *Little Flowers of St. Francis* or Maurus and

Placid in the *Life of St. Benedict,* these disciples of Columba serve as foils or reliefs against which the divine power of the saint is portrayed. Two in particular should be noted: Baithene, Columba's beloved disciple who is present for many of his miracles and who will succeed him as Abbot of Iona; and Diormit, Columba's personal assistant who witnessed many secret manifestations of divine power the other monks are not privy to.

The *Cathach* of Saint Columba

Before we move on from St. Columba, we must say a word about the famed *Cathach* of St. Columba, the most enduring relic of the saint of Iona.

The *Cathach* is a psalter containing at present 58 folio pages containing Psalms 30:13 through 105:13. The text is the Gallican version of the Latin Vulgate. The document has been dated to around the late 6th century and is believed to have been written by the hand of Columba himself. It is the second oldest Latin manuscript in Ireland, and the second oldest Latin psalter in the entire world.

Given its antiquity, the *Cathach* stands as one of the patriarchal texts of medieval illuminations, crafted right at the dawning of the practice. It is written in something called Insular script, a monastic handwriting that developed in Ireland and was an influence upon the later Carolingian miniscule. Compared to later illuminated manuscripts, the decorations in the *Cathach* are scarce, limited to the first letter of each psalm (the drop-cap M on the back cover of this book is taken from the *Cathach*). Each of these first letters is written with a thick black stroke decorated with trumpet and spiral patterns, in addition to a design known as guilloche, the intricate, repetitive patterns Celtic art is known for. Unfortunately, the front page and many other pages of the psalter have been lost. The entire psalter was written by a single scribe;

the thick downstrokes and thin horizontals suggest the scribe used an edged rather than a pointed quill. If the tradition is to be believed—and the dating of the artifact suggests no reason why it should not be—then we are looking at the very handwriting of St. Columba himself.

The word *Cathach* means "Battler." This refers to the extraordinary way the Irish used this document. At some time early in its history, the *Cathach* came into possession of the Clan O'Donnell of County Donegal, the old royal family of Tír Chonaill. The O'Donnells carried the Cathach into battle, using it as a rallying point, as well as a relic believed to grant protection and victory to O'Donnell armies. The *Cathach* was borne into battle according to a specific ritual: it could only be borne by a monk or holy man of the Clan McGroarty; its bearer had to be sinless and have a reputation for holiness; the *Cathach* was enclosed in a special leather satchel known as a *tiag* (and later in a box called a *cumdach*) and attached to the neck of the bearer; the bearer then processed in a circle around the O'Donnell troops three times before battle. The *Cathach* was in continuous use by the O'Donnells until 1497, when its keeper Mac Robhartaigh was slain in the Battle of Bealach Buidhe, near Boyne.

Sometime between 1062 and 1098 the *Cathach* was enclosed inside a special box called a cumdach. The cumdach of the *Cathach* is an oblong hinged wooden box, decorated with bronze and gilt-silver plates with mounts holding glass and crystal settings. The sides of the cumdach feature Ringerike decorations, a style of Viking art reflecting the Norse influence in Ireland in the latter first millennium. In the late 14th century, a new face was made in gilt repoussé depicting Christ enthroned flanked by a scene of the crucifixion on the right and an image of St. Columba to the left.

After the O'Donnells lost the *Cathach* at the Battle of Bealach Buidhe the relic changed hands several times before finding its way back to the Clan O'Donnell in the person of Daniel O'Donell

(1666-1735), a captain in the army of King James II of England who later became a Brigadier-General in the Irish Brigade of France. Daniel O'Donnell had special devotion to the *Cathach*, believing in its powers and traditional associations with the Clan O'Donnell. In 1732, while O'Donnell was in Paris during his service in the French army he had extensive repairs made to the *Cathach* by French artisans. Shortly after this, O'Donnell fell ill. Knowing death was approaching, he deposited the relic inside a silver box and entrusted it to a Belgian monastery with strict instructions that the sacred object should only be handed over to him who could prove himself chief of the O'Donnells.

There it remained for over sixty years until 1802 when Sir Neale O'Donnell, 2nd Baronet of Newport House, County Mayo, was able to claim the *Cathach*. It was returned to Ireland, and Sir Neale's son, Sir Richard, donated the *Cathach* to the Royal Irish Academy in 1842. Unfortunately, the *Cathach* and cumdach were separated shortly thereafter, the cumdach going to the archaeology department of the National Museum of Ireland while the *Cathach* itself remained in the Royal Irish Academy. Until 1920, the leaves of the *Cathach* were stuck together, but the painstaking work of researchers at the British Museum separated them, allowing them to be read for the first time in centuries. Further restorations were carried out in 1980-81.

Notes on the English Text

The text is that of the English translation published in Edinburgh in 1874 by Edmonston and Douglas, edited by William Reeves. We have remained faithful to this translation, with a few caveats. The biggest change has been in our rendering of the name of the island of Iona. In Adomnán's original Latin, Iona is always referred to as "Ioua insula," literally, "the Iouan island." Every time this phrase appears, the Reeves translation of 1874 renders it cumbersomely "the Iouan island (Hy, now Iona)." The parenthetical "Hy, now Iona" is an attempt to include the nomenclature of St. Bede in his *Historia ecclesiastica gentis Anglorum,* who refers to the island as Hy or Hii. We believed this to be too much of a disruption in the narrative and have opted to simply translate "Ioua insula" as "the island of Iona" or simply "Iona." Other than this, we have left in all the parenthetical place name indicators included by Reeves in order to help the reader connect the places mentioned in the text with their modern counterparts.

Two other notes: In certain places "thee", "thou", and "thy" have been rendered into their contemporary forms where we thought it would aid comprehension; in other places they are retained where we thought their meaning was clear. The only other alteration was in some of the chapter headings, which we felt were occasionally too verbose. For example, the original title of Book Three Chapter 20 was "Of the angelic splendour of the light which Virgnous, a youth of good disposition, and afterwards made by God superior of this Church in which I, though unworthy, now serve-saw coming down upon St. Columba in the Church, on a winter's night, when the brethren were at rest in their chambers." These sorts of lengthy chapter headings have occasionally been reduced.

Irish Catholicism in the time of Columba provided a vital link between the Church of the patristic era and the Christian civilization of the Middle Ages. St. Columba served as "the pillar of many churches"[27] in nourishing this unique culture, the union of the native Irish genius forged by Christian revelation. It is our hope that this new edition of Adomnán's *Vita Columbae* will rekindle interest in the life of this important saint, as well as call to mind the oft forgotten lives of many of the great *sancti obscuri* of the early Middle Ages.

St. Columba, St. Adomnán, and all the glorious saints of Éire, look kindly on this humble work and remember us before the throne of God.

Introduction Notes

1 Book III:3
2 Book I: 24
3 Book II:26
4 Book II:1
5 For example, Book I:6 and I:14.
6 Book II:8
7 Book I:19
8 Book III:24
9 Book III:4
10 Book I:7-8
11 Book III:6
12 Book II:36
13 Book I:1
14 Book II:34-35
15 Book III:24
16 Book III:6
17 Book III:24
18 Adomnán mentions that another work was written on St. Columba by someone named "Cummene the Fair", which clearly predated Adomnán's Vita since he cites it in Book III, Chap. 6. Whoever this Cummene was has been lost to history, along with his work.
19 Book II:46
20 St. Bede, Historia ecclesiastica gentis Anglorum, Book V:15
21 Book II:46
22 Book I:35
23 Book III:20
24 Book I:34
25 Bonaventure, *Legenda maior*, chapter 5
26 Book I:3
27 Book III:24

Book One
Prophetic Revelations
of Saint Columba

Chapter 1
A Brief Narrative of Saint Columba's Miracles

According to the promise given above, I shall commence this book with a brief account of the evidences which the venerable man gave of his power. By virtue of his prayer, and in the name of our Lord Jesus Christ, he healed several persons suffering under various diseases; and he alone, by the assistance of God, expelled from this our island,[1] which now has the primacy, innumerable hosts of malignant spirits, whom he saw with his bodily eyes assailing himself, and beginning to bring deadly distempers on his monastic brotherhood. Partly by mortification, and partly by a bold resistance, he subdued, with the help of Christ, the furious rage of wild beasts. The surging waves, also, at times rolling mountains high in a great tempest, became quickly at his prayer quiet and smooth, and his ship, in which he then happened to be, reached the desired haven in a perfect calm.

When returning from the country of the Picts,[2] where he had been for some days, he hoisted his sail when the breeze was against him to confound the Druids, and made as rapid a voyage as if the wind had been favorable. On other occasions, also, contrary winds were at his prayers changed into fair. In that same country, he took a white stone from the river, and blessed it for the working of certain cures, and that stone, contrary to nature, floated like an apple when placed in water. This divine miracle was wrought in the presence of King Brude and his household.[3]

In the same country, also, he performed a still greater miracle, by raising to life the dead child of a humble believer, and restoring him in life and vigor to his father and mother.

At another time, while the blessed man was yet a young deacon in Hibernia, residing with the holy bishop Findbarr,[4] the wine required for the sacred mysteries failed, and he changed by his prayer pure water into true wine.

An immense blaze of heavenly light was on many and wholly distinct occasions seen by some of the brethren to surround him in the light of day, as well as in the darkness of the night. He was also favored with the sweet and most delightful society of bright hosts of the holy angels. He often saw, by the revelation of the Holy Ghost, the souls of some just men carried by angels to the highest heavens. And the reprobates too he very frequently beheld carried to hell by demons.

He very often foretold the future deserts, sometimes joyful, and sometimes sad, of many persons while they were still living in mortal flesh. In the dreadful crash of wars he obtained from God, by the virtue of prayer that some kings should be conquered, and others come off victorious.

And such a grace as this he enjoyed, not only while alive in this world, but even after his departure from the flesh, as God, from whom all the saints derive their honor, has made him still a victorious and most valiant champion in battle. I shall give one example of especial honor conferred by Almighty God on this honorable man, the event having occurred the day before the Saxon prince Oswald went forth to fight with Catlon, a very valiant king of the Britons.[5] For as this same King Oswald, after pitching his camp, in readiness for the battle, was sleeping one day on a pillow in his tent, he saw St. Columba in a vision, beaming with angelic brightness, and of figure so majestic that his head seemed to touch the clouds. The blessed man having announced his name to the king, stood in the midst of the camp, and covered it all with his brilliant garment, except at one small distant point; and at the same time he uttered those cheering words which the Lord spoke to Joshua son of Nun before the passage of the Jordan, after Moses' death, saying, "Be strong and of a good courage; behold, I shall be with thee," etc. [Jos. 1:9] Then St. Columba having said these words to the king in the vision, added, "March out this following night from your camp to battle, for on this occasion the Lord has granted to me that your foes shall be put to flight, that your enemy Catlon shall be delivered into your hands, and that after the battle you shall return in triumph, and have a happy reign."

The king, awaking at these words, assembled his council and related the vision, at which they were all encouraged; and so the whole people promised that, after their return from the war, they would believe and be baptized, for up to that time all that Saxon land had been wrapped in the darkness of paganism and ignorance, with the exception of King Oswald and the twelve men who had been baptized with him during his exile among the Scots. What more need I say? On the very next night, King Oswald, as he had been directed in the vision, went forth from his camp to battle, and had a much smaller army than the numerous hosts opposed to him, yet he obtained from the Lord, according to His promise, an easy and decisive victory, for King Catlon was slain, and the conqueror, on his return after the battle, was ever after established by God as the Bretwalda of all Britain.[6] I, Adomnán, had this narrative from the lips of my predecessor, the Abbot

Failbe, who solemnly declared that he had himself heard King Oswald relating this same vision to Segine the abbot.

But another fact must not be omitted, that by some poems composed in the Scotic language[7] in praise of the same blessed man, and by the commemoration of his name, certain wicked men of lewd conversation, and men of blood, were saved from the hands of their enemies, who in the night had surrounded the house in which they were singing these hymns. They safely escaped through the flames, the swords, and the spears; and, strange to tell, a few of those only who despised these commemorations of the holy man, and refused to join in the hymns, perished in that assault of the enemy. It is not two or three witnesses, as the law requires, but even hundreds and more, that could be cited in proof of this miracle. Nor is it in one place or on one occasion only that the same is known to have happened, but even at different times and places, in both Scotia (Ireland) and Britain, it is proved beyond all doubt that the like security was obtained, in the same manner and by the same means. I have learned this for certain, from well-informed men in those very countries where similar miracles have taken place.

But, to return to the point in hand: among the miracles which this same man of the Lord, while dwelling in mortal flesh, performed by the gift of God, was his foretelling the future by the spirit of prophecy, with which he was highly favored from his early years, and making known to those who were present what was happening in other places: for though absent in body he was present in spirit, and could look on things that were widely apart, according to the words of St. Paul, "He that is joined unto the Lord is one spirit."

Hence this same man of the Lord, St. Columba, when a few of the brethren would sometimes inquire into the matter, did not deny but that by some divine intuition, and through a wonderful expansion of his inner soul, he beheld the whole universe drawn together and laid open to his sight, as in one ray of the sun.

This account of the miracles of the holy men I have given here for this purpose, that my reader, in this brief sketch, may have a foretaste of the richer banquet which is before him, in the fuller narrative which is to be given, with the assistance of the Lord, in the three following books. Here it appears to me not improper, though it may be out of the usual order, to record some prophecies which the blessed man gave at different times, regarding certain holy and illustrious men.

Chapter 2
Of Saint Finten the Abbot, Son of Tailchan[8]

St. Finten, who was afterwards very well known throughout all the churches of the Scots, having, by the grace of God, preserved from his boyhood purity of body and soul, and being devoted to the study of divine wisdom, had nourished from his youthful years this one resolve in his heart, that he would leave Hibernia and go abroad to St. Columba. Burning with that desire, he went to an old friend, the most prudent and venerable cleric in his country, who was called in the Scotic tongue Columb Crag, to get some sound advice from him. When he had laid open his mind to him, he received the following answer: "As thy devout wish is, I feel, inspired by God, who can presume to say that thou should not cross the sea to St. Columba?" At the same moment two monks of St. Columba happened to arrive, and when they were asked about their journey, they replied: "We have lately come across from Britain, and to-day we have come from the Oakwood of Calgach[9]." "Is he well," says Columb Crag, "your holy father Columba?"

Then they burst into tears, and answered with great sorrow, "Our patron is indeed well, for a few days ago he departed to

Christ." Hearing this, Finten and Columb, and all who were there present, fell on their faces on the ground, and wept bitterly. Finten then asked, "Whom did he leave as his successor?"

"Baithene, his disciple," they replied. And as all cried out, "It is meet and right," Columb said to Finten, "What will you now do, Finten?"

He answered, "With God's permission, I will sail over to Baithene, that wise and holy man, and if he receive me I will take him as my abbot." Then kissing the aforementioned Columb, and bidding him farewell, he prepared for his voyage, and setting sail without the least delay, arrived at Iona.[10] As up to that time his name was wholly unknown in those places, he was only received at first with the hospitality given to every unknown stranger; but next day he sent a messenger to Baithene, and asked to have a personal interview. Baithene, ever kind and affable to strangers, ordered him to be introduced. Being at once brought in, he first, as seemed meet, knelt down upon the ground; and then being ordered by the holy abbot to rise and be seated, he was asked by Baithene, who as yet knew nothing of his family, province, name, or life, what was his motive for encountering the labor of the voyage. In reply to the inquiry thus made he told everything in order, and then humbly asked to be admitted. The holy abbot, hearing these things from his guest, and recognizing him at the same time as the man of whom St. Columba had some time previously made a prophecy, replied: "Truly, my son, I ought to give thanks to my God for thy arrival, but be thou assured of this, that you will not be one of our monks."

On hearing this, the stranger was very much grieved, and said: "Perhaps I am unworthy to become thy monk." "It is not because thou art unworthy, as you say, that I gave that answer," immediately replied the abbot, "for I would indeed prefer retaining you with me, but I cannot disobey the command of

St. Columba, my predecessor, by whom the Holy Ghost prophesied of thee. For, as I was alone with him one day, among other things which he foretold was the following: 'Hearken very attentively, O Baithene,' said he, 'to these my words, for shortly after my welcome and earnestly longed-for departure from this world to Christ, a certain brother from Scotia, named Finten, son of Tailchan, of the tribe Mocumoie, who is now carefully guarding his youthful years with a good life, and is very well versed in sacred studies, will, I say, come to thee, and humbly ask thee to receive and enroll him with your other monks. But this has not been appointed for him in the foreknowledge of God that he should become the monk of any abbot, for he has long since been chosen of God to be an abbot of monks and a leader of souls to the kingdom of heaven. Thou shalt not therefore detain that illustrious man with thee on these islands of ours, lest you should even seem to oppose the will of God, but you shall make known to him what I have told thee, and send him back in peace to Scotia, that he may found a monastery in the parts of the Leinstermen, near the sea, and that there feeding the flock of Christ, he shall lead a countless host of souls to their heavenly country.'"

The holy youth hearing this burst into tears, and returning thanks to Christ, said: "Be it unto me according to the prophecy and wonderful foreknowledge of St. Columba." At the same time, in obedience to the words of the saints, he received the blessing of Baithene, and sailed back in peace to Scotia.

I have heard this as an undoubted fact from the lips of an aged and pious priest and soldier of Christ, called Oissene, son of Ernan, of the tribe Mocu Neth Corb, who averred that he had himself heard these very words from the lips of St. Finten, son of Tailchan, whose monk he himself had been.

Chapter 3
Prophecy of Saint Columba Regarding Ernene

On another occasion, while the blessed man was residing for a few months in the midland part of Hibernia, when founding by divine inspiration his monastery, which in the Scotic tongue is called Dair-mag (Durrow), was pleased to pay a visit to the brethren who dwelt in St. Ceran's monastery, Clon (Clonmacnoise). As soon as it was known that he was near, all flocked from their little grange farms near the monastery, and, along with those who were within it, ranged themselves, with enthusiasm, under the abbot Alither; then advancing beyond the enclosure of the monastery, they went out as one man to meet St. Columba, as if he were an angel of the Lord. Humbly bowing down, with their faces to the ground, in his presence, they kissed him most reverently, and singing hymns of praise as they went they conducted him with all honor to the Church. Over the saint, as he walked, a canopy made of wood was supported by four men walking by his side, lest the holy abbot, St. Columba, should be troubled by the crowd of brethren pressing upon him.

At that very time, a boy attached to the monastery, who was mean in dress and look, and hitherto had not stood well in the opinions of the seniors, concealing himself as well as he could, came forward stealthily, that he might touch unperceived even the hem of the cloak which the blessed man wore, without his feeling or knowing it. This, however, did not escape the saint, for he knew with the eyes of his soul what he could not see taking place behind him with the eyes of his body. Stopping therefore suddenly, and putting out his hand behind him, he seized the boy by the neck, and bringing him round set him before his face. The crowd of bystanders cried out: "Let him go, let him go: why do you touch that unfortunate and naughty boy?" But the saint solemnly uttered these prophetic words from his pure heart: "Suffer it to be so now, brethren;" then turning to the boy, who was in the greatest terror, he said, "My son, open thy mouth, and put out thy tongue." The boy did as he was bid, and in great alarm opened his mouth and put out his tongue: the saint extended to it his holy hand, and after carefully blessing it pronounced his prophecy in the following words: "Though this boy appears to you now very contemptible and worthless, let no one on that account despise him. For from this hour, not only will he not displease you, but he will give you every satisfaction; from day to day he shall advance by degrees in good conduct, and in the virtues of the soul; from this day, wisdom and prudence shall be more and more increased in him, and great shall be his progress in this your community: his tongue also shall receive from God the gift of both wholesome doctrine and eloquence." This was Ernene, son of Crasen, who was afterwards famous and most highly honored in all the churches of Scotia (Ireland). He himself told all these words which were prophesied regarding himself, as written above, to the abbot Segine, in the attentive hearing of my predecessor Failbe, who was present at the time with Segine, and from whose lips I myself have come to know all that I have stated.

But during this short time that the saint was a guest in the monastery of Clon, there were many other things also which he prophesied by the revelation of the Holy Ghost; as, for instance, about the discord which arose a long time after among the churches of Scotia, on account of the difference with regard to the Easter Feast; and about some visits of angels distinctly made to himself, certain places within the enclosure of the monastery being at that time thus resorted to by the angels.

Chapter 4
Of the Prophesied Arrival of Saint Cainnech

At another time, on Iona, on a day when the tempest was fierce and the sea was exceedingly boisterous, the saint, as he sat in the house, gave orders to his brethren, saying, "Prepare the guest-chamber quickly, and draw water to wash the strangers' feet." One of the brethren upon this inquired: "Who can cross the Sound safely, narrow though it be, on so perilous and stormy a day?" The saint, on hearing this, thus made answer, "The Almighty has given a calm even in this tempest to a certain holy and excellent man, who will arrive here among us before evening." And lo! The same day, the ship for which the brethren had some time been looking out arrived, according to the saint's prediction, and brought St. Cainnech.[11] The saint went forth with the brethren to meet him and received him with all honour and hospitality. But the sailors who had been with St. Cainnech, when they were asked by the brethren what sort of a voyage they had had, told them, even as St. Columba had predicted, about both the tempest and the calm which God had given in the same sea and at the same time, with an amazing distinction between the two. The tempest they saw at a distance, yet they said they did not feel it.

Chapter 5
Of the Danger to the Holy Bishop Columbanus in the Sea

On another day; also, while St. Columba was engaged in his mother-church, he suddenly cried out, with a smile, "Columbanus, the son of Beogna, has just now set out on a voyage to us, and is in great danger in the rolling tides of Brecan's whirlpool: he is sitting at the prow and raising both his hands to heaven: he is also blessing that angry and dreadful sea: yet in this the Lord only frightens him, for the ship in which he is shall not be wrecked in the storm; but this is rather to excite him to pray more fervently, that by God's favor he may escape the danger of his voyage, and reach us in safety."

Chapter 6
Of Cormac

On another occasion also St. Columba prophesied in the following manner of Cormac, grandson of Lethan, a truly pious man, who not less than three times went in search of a desert in the ocean, but did not find it.[12] "In his desire to find a desert, Cormac is this day, for the second time, now embarking from that district which lies at the other side of the river Moda (the Moy, in Sligo), and is called Eirros, Domno (Erris, in Mayo); nor even this time shall he find what he seeks, and that for no other fault than that he has irregularly allowed to accompany him in the voyage a monk who is going away from his own proper abbot without obtaining his consent."

Chapter 7
Columba's Prophecies of Battles Fought at a Distance

About two years, as we have been told, after the battle of Cule-Drebene (in Connaught), at which time the blessed man first set sail and took his departure from Scotia (Ireland), it happened that on the very day and at the same hour when the battle, called in Scotic Ondemone (near Coleraine), was fought in Scotia, the same man of God was then living in Britain with King Connall, the son of Comgell, and told him everything, as well about the battle itself, as also about those kings to whom the Lord granted the victory over their enemies. These kings were known as Ainmore, son of Setna, and the two sons of Mac Erca, Domnall and Forcus. And the saint, in like manner, prophesied of the king of the Cruithne, who was called Echoid Laib, and how, after being defeated, he escaped riding in his chariot.

On the Battle *of the Miathi*

At another time, after the lapse of many years from the above-mentioned battle, and while the holy man was at Iona, he suddenly said to his minister, Diormit, "Ring the bell!" The brethren, startled at the sound, proceeded quickly to the church, with the holy prelate himself at their head. There he began, on bended knees, to say to them, "Let us pray now earnestly to the Lord for this people and King Aidan,[13] for they are engaging in battle at this moment." Then after a short time he went out of the oratory, and, looking up to heaven, said, "The barbarians are fleeing now, and to Aidan is given the victory, a sad one though it be." And the blessed man in his prophecy declared the number of the slain in Aidan's army to be three hundred and three men.

Chapter 8
Prophecy Regarding the Sons of King Aidan

At another time, before the above-mentioned battle, the saint asked King Aidan about his successor to the crown. The king answered that of his three sons, Artur, Eochoid Find, and Domingart, he knew not which would have the kingdom after him. Then at once the saint prophesied on this wise, "None of these three shall be king, for they shall fall in battle, slain by their enemies; but now if thou hast any younger sons, let them come to me, and that one of them whom the Lord has chosen to be king will at once rush into my lap." When they were called in, Eochoid Buide, according to the word of the saint, advanced and rested in his bosom. Immediately the saint kissed him, and, giving him his blessing, said to his father, "This one: shall survive and reign as king after thee, and his sons shall reign after him." And so were all these things fully accomplished afterwards in their time. For

Artur and Eochoid Find were not long after killed in the above-mentioned battle of the Miathi; Domingart was also defeated and slain in battle in Saxonia; while Eochoid Buide succeeded his father on the throne.

Of Domnall, Son of Aid

Domnall, son of Aid, while yet a boy, was brought by those who brought him up to St. Columba on the ridge of Ceatt (Druim Ceatt in Londonderry), who looked at him and inquired, "Whose son is this whom you have brought here?" They answered, "This is Domnall, son of Aid, who is brought to thee for this purpose, that he may return enriched by thy blessing." The saint blessed him immediately and said. "He shall survive all his brethren, and be a very famous king, nor shall he be ever delivered into the hands of his enemies; but in his old age, in his own house, and with a crowd of his familiar friends around him, he shall die peacefully in his bed." All this was truly fulfilled in him, as the blessed man had foretold.

Of Scandlan, Son of Colman

At the same time and place, the saint, wishing to visit Scandlan, son of Colman, went to him where he was kept in prison by King Aid, and when he had blessed him he comforted him, saying, "Son, do not distress yourself, but rather rejoice and take courage, for King Aid, who has you a prisoner, will go out of this world before you, and after some time of exile you shall reign in your own nation for thirty years. And again you shall be driven from your kingdom, and be in exile for some days; but after that you shall be called home again by your people, and shall reign for three short terms." All this was fully accomplished according to the prediction of the saint. For in thirty years he had to leave his throne, and continued in exile for some time; and then being recalled by his people, he reigned not three years, as he expected, but three months, and at the end of that time he died.

A Prophecy of Columba Regarding Two Other Kings

At another time, while travelling through the rough and rocky country which is called Artdamuirchol (Ardnamurchan), he heard his companions Laisran, son of Feradach, and Diormit, his minister, speaking on the way of the two above-named kings, and addressed them in these words, "O my dear children, why do you talk thus foolishly of these men? Both of these kings of whom you are now conversing are newly slain, and have had their heads cut off by their enemies. And this very day some sailors shall come here from Scotia (Ireland), and tell you the same about these kings." That same day some sailors arrived from Hibernia, at a place which is called Muirbolc Paradisi (Portnamurloch in Lismore), and told the two above-named companions, who were now sailing in the same ship with the saint, how these kings had been slain, and thus the prophecy of the venerable man fulfilled.

Prophecy Regarding Oingus, Son of Aid Comman

When he and his two brothers were driven from his country, he came as an exile to the saint, who was then wandering in Britain, and who, in blessing him, uttered these prophetic words from his holy heart, "This youth shall survive when his other brothers are gone, and he shall reign a long time in his native country; his enemies shall fall before him, while he shall never fall into their hands, but in old age he shall die peacefully in the midst of his friends." All this was fully accomplished according to the saint's words. This was Oingus, surnamed Bronbachal.

Prophecy Regarding the Son of King Dermit

On another occasion, when the blessed man was sojourning for some days in Ireland, he spoke in the following prophetic strain to the above-mentioned Aid, who had come to visit him: "You must take care, my son, lest, for the sin of murdering your kinsman, you lose the right of governing the whole of Ireland, as was first assigned you by God; for if at any time you commit that sin, you shall not hold the whole of your father's kingdom, but only a part of it in your own tribe, and that but for a short time." These words of the saint were on this wise fulfilled according to the prediction, that after Aid had treacherously killed Suitne, son of Columban, he reigned, it is said, no longer than four years and three months, and that only as colleague in the kingdom.

Prophecy of the Blessed Man Regarding King Roderc

This same king being on friendly terms with the holy man, sent to him on one occasion a secret message by Lugbe Mocumin, as he was anxious to know whether he would be killed by his enemies or not. But when Lugte was being closely inquired at by the saint regarding the king, his kingdom, and people, he answered in a tone of pity, "Why do you ask about that wretched man, who is quite unable to tell at what hour he may be killed by his enemies?"

Then the saint replied, "He shall never be delivered into the hands of his enemies; he will die at home on his own pillow." And the prophecy of the saint regarding King Roderc was fully accomplished; for, according to his word, he died quietly in his own house.

Chapter 9
Prophecy of the Saint Regarding two Boys

On another occasion, two men of low rank in life came to the saint, who was then on the Island of Iona. One of them, named Meldan, brought his son to the saint and asked him what kind of future he would enjoy. To whom the saint replied, "Is not this the Sabbath day? Your son will die on the sixth day at the end of next week, and will be buried here on the eighth day, that is the Sabbath." Then the other man, named Glasderc, also took his son along with him, and venturing to make a similar inquiry, received the following answer from the saint, "Thy son Ernan will see his grandchildren, and be buried in old age in this island." All this was fully accomplished in its own time regarding the two boys, according to the words of the saint.

Chapter 10
Prophecy Regarding Colca, Son of Aid Draignich

This Colca residing one time in the Island of Iona with the saint, was asked by him concerning his mother whether she was a pious woman or not. Colca answered him, "I have always known my mother to be good, and to bear that character." The saint then spoke these prophetic words: "Set out now at once for Scotia (Ireland), with God's help, and question your mother closely regarding her very grievous secret sin, which she will not confess to any man." To carry out the advice thus given him he departed to Hibernia: and when he interrogated his mother closely, she at first denied, and then she at last confessed her sin. When she had done penance according to the judgment of the saint, she was absolved, wondering very much all the while at what was made known to the saint regarding her.

Chapter 11
More Concerning Colca

Colca, however, returned to the saint, and remained with him for some days, and then asking about the end of his own days, received this answer from the saint: "In thine own beloved country you shall be head of a church for many years, and when at any time you happen to see thy butler making merry with a company of his friends at supper, and twirling the ladle round in the strainer, know that then in a short time you shall die." What more need I say? This same prophecy of the blessed man was exactly fulfilled as it was foretold to Colca.

Chapter 12
Regarding Laisrean, the Gardener, a Holy Man

One day, the holy man ordered one of his monks named Trena, of the tribe Mocuruntir, to take a message for him to Ireland. While he was preparing the ship in haste to obey the orders of the man of God, he complained before the saint that one of the sailors was missing. The saint immediately answered him and uttered these words from his sacred breast, "The sailor who is, you say, absent, I cannot just now find. But go in peace; thou shalt have a favorable and steady breeze till thou reach Hibernia. Thou shalt see a man coming to meet thee from a distance, and he will be the first to seize the prow of thy ship in Ireland; he shall be with thee during the time of thy sojourn in Hibernia, and accompany thee on thy return to us, as a man chosen by God, who in this very monastery of mine will live piously the remainder of his days." What more can I add? Trena received the saint's blessing, and crossed over at full sail during the whole voyage, and lo! as his little ship was nearing the port, Laisran Mocumoie ran forward before the others and caught the prow. The sailors knew that this was the very man of whom the saint had spoken beforehand.

Chapter 13
How the Saint Knew Beforehand About a Great Whale

One day when the venerable man was staying in Island of Iona, a certain brother named Berach intended to sail to the Ethican island (Tiree), and going to the saint in the morning asked his blessing. The saint looking at him, said, "O my son, take very great care this day not to attempt sailing direct over the open sea to the Ethican land; but rather take a circuit, and sail round by the smaller islands, for this reason, that thou be not thrown into great terror by a huge monster, and hardly be able to escape." On receiving the saint's blessing he departed, and when he reached his ship, he set sail without giving heed to the saint's words. But as he was crossing over the larger arms of the Ethican sea, he and the sailors who were with him looked out, and lo, a whale, of huge and amazing size, raised itself like a mountain, and as it floated on the surface, it opened its mouth, which, as it gaped; was bristling with teeth. Then the rowers, hauling in their sail, pulled back in the utmost terror, and had a very narrow escape from the agitation of the waves caused by the motion of the monster; and they were also struck with wonder as they remembered the prophetic words of the saint.

On the morning of that same day, as Baithene was going to sail to the forenamed island, the saint told him about this whale, saying, "Last night, at midnight, a great whale rose from the depth of the sea, and it will float this day on the surface of the ocean between Iona and the Ethican islands (Iona and Tiree)." Baithene answered and said, "That beast and I are under the power of God." "Go in peace," said the saint, "thy faith in Christ shall defend thee from this danger." Baithene accordingly, having received the saint's blessing, sailed from the harbor; and after they had sailed a considerable distance, he and his companions saw the whale; and while all the others were much terrified, he alone was without fear, and raising up both his hands, blessed the sea and the whale. At the same moment the enormous brute plunged down under the waves, and never afterwards appeared to them.

Chapter 14
Prophecy Regarding a Certain Baitan, who With Others Sailed in Search of a Desert in the Ocean[14]

At another time, a certain man named Baitan, by race a descendant of Niath Taloirc, when setting out with others to seek a desert in the sea, asked the saint's blessing. The saint bidding him adieu uttered this prophecy regarding him: "This man who is going in search of a desert in the ocean shall not be buried in the desert, but in that place where a woman shall drive sheep over his grave." The same Baitan, after long wanderings on stormy seas, returned to his native country without finding the desert, and remained for many years the head of a small monastic house, which is called in the Scotic tongue Lathreginden. When after a while he died and was buried, in the Oakgrove of Galgach (Derry), it happened at the same time that on account of some hostile inroad the poor people with their wives and children fled for sanctuary to the church of that place. Whence it occurred that on a certain day a woman was caught, as she was driving her lambs over the grave of this same man who was newly buried. Then a holy priest who was present and saw this, said, "Now is fulfilled the prophecy which St. Columba uttered many years ago!' And this I myself was told regarding Baitan, by that same priest and soldier of Christ, Mailodran by name, of the tribe of Mocurin.

Chapter 15
Prophecy Regarding Neman, a False Penitent

At another time, the saint came to the Hinbina island (Eilean-na-naoimh, one of the Garveloch Islands), and that same day he gave orders that even the penitents[15] should enjoy some indulgence in respect of their food. Now there was among the penitents in that place a certain Neman, son of Cathair, who, though ordered by the saint, declined to accept the offer of this little indulgence. Him then the saint addressed in these words: "O Neman, are you not accepting some indulgence in food as it is kindly granted by me and Baitan? The time shall come when you will be stealthily eating mare's flesh as you lay concealed in the woods with robbers." And accordingly that same man afterwards returned to the world, and was found in a forest with robbers taking and eating off a wooden griddle such flesh as the saint had foretold.

Chapter 16
Regarding an Unhappy Man Who Lay With His Mother

At another time, the saint called out the brethren at the dead of night, and when they were assembled in the church said to them: "Now let us pray fervently to the Lord, for at this hour a sin unheard of in the world has been committed, for which rigorous vengeance that is justly due is very much to be feared." The next day he spoke of this sin to a few who were asking him about it. "After a few months," he said, "that unhappy wretch will come here to the Iona with Lugaid, who is unaware of the sin." Accordingly after the few months had passed away, the saint one day spoke to Diormit, and ordered him, "Rise quickly; lo! Lugaid is coming. Tell him to send off the wretch whom he has with him in the ship to the Malean island (Mull), that he may not tread the sod of this island." He went to the sea in obedience to the saint's injunction, and told Lugaid as he was approaching all the words of the saint regarding the unhappy man. On hearing the directions, that unhappy man vowed that he would never eat food with others until he had seen St. Columba and spoken to him. Diormit therefore returned to the saint, and told him the words of the poor wretch. The saint, on hearing them, went down to the haven, and as Baitan was citing the authority of Holy Scriptures, and suggesting that the repentance of the unhappy man should be received, the saint immediately replied to him, "O Baitan! This man has committed fratricide like Cain, and become an adulterer with his mother." Then the poor wretch, casting himself upon his knees on the beach, promised that he would comply with all the rules of penance, according to the judgment of the saint. The saint said to him, "If you do penance in tears and lamentations for twelve years among the Britons and never to the day of thy death return to Scotia (Ireland), perhaps God may pardon thy sin." Having said these words, the saint turned to his own friends and said, "This man is a son of perdition, who will not perform the penance he has promised, but will soon return to Scotia (Ireland), and there in a short time be killed by his enemies." All this happened exactly according to the saint's prophecy; for the wretched man, returning to Hibernia about the same time, fell into the hands of his enemies in the region called Lea (Firli, in Ulster), and was murdered. He was of the descendants of Turtre.

Chapter 17
Of the Vowel 'I'

One day Baithene came to the saint and said, "I want some one of the brethren to look over with me and correct the psalter which I have written."

Hearing this, the saint said, "Why give us this trouble without any cause? In that psalter of thine, of which you speak, there is not one superfluous letter to be found, nor is any wanting except the one vowel I." And accordingly, when the whole psalter was read over, what the saint had said was found to be true.

Chapter 18
Of the Book Which Fell Into the Water-Vessel,
as Saint Columba had foretold

In the same way, on another day, as he was sitting by the hearth in the monastery, he saw at some distance Lugbe, of the tribe Mocumin, reading a book, and suddenly said to him, "Take care, my son, take care, for I think that the book you read is about to fall into a vessel full of water." And so it soon happened, for when the same youth rose soon after to perform some duty in the monastery, he forgot the word of the blessed man, and the book which he held negligently under his arm suddenly fell into the water-pot, which was full of water.

Chapter 19
Of the Inkhorn, Awkwardly Spilled

On another day a shout was given on the other side of the Sound of Iona. The saint hearing the shout, as he was sitting in his little hut, which was made of planks, said, "The man who is shouting beyond the Sound is not of very sharp wit, for when he is here today he will upset my inkhorn and spill the ink." Diormit, his minister, hearing this, stood a little in front of the door, and waited for the arrival of this troublesome guest, in order to save the inkhorn. But for some cause or other he had soon to leave his place, and after his departure the unwelcome guest arrived; in his eager haste to kiss the saint, he upset the inkhorn with the hem of his garment and spilled the ink.

Chapter 20
Of the Arrival of Another Guest Foretold by the Saint

So again at another time the saint spoke thus to his brethren on the third day of the week, "We intend to fast tomorrow, being

Wednesday: and yet by the arrival of a certain troublesome guest the usual fast will be broken." And so it happened as had been shown to the saint beforehand; for on the morning of that same Wednesday, another stranger was heard signaling across the Sound. This was Aidan, the son of Fergno, who, it is said, was minister for twelve years to Brendan Mocualti. He was a very religious man, and his arrival, as the saint had foretold, broke the fast of that day.

Chapter 21
Of a Man in Distress Who Was Crying Across the Sound

On another day the saint heard some person shouting across the Sound, and said, "That man who is shouting is much to be pitied, for he is coming here to us to ask some cure for the disease of his body; but it were better for him this day to do true penance for his sins, for at the close of this week he shall die." These words those who were present told to the unhappy man when he arrived. But he gave no heed to them when he had received what he asked, and quickly departed, yet before the end of the same week he died, according to the prediction of the saint.

Chapter 22
The Prophecy of Saint Columba Regarding the Roman City, Burnt By Fire Which Fell From Heaven

Another time also, Lugbe, of the tribe Mocumin, of whom I spoke already, came to the saint one day after the grinding of the corn, but the saint's countenance shone with such wonderful brilliance that he could not look upon it, and quickly fled in great terror. The saint gently clapped his hands and called him back; then on his return the saint asked him why he fled so quickly. "I fled," he replied, "because I was very much alarmed." Then becoming more confident, after a while, he ventured to ask the saint, "Has some awful vision been shown to thee just now?" The saint answered, "A very fearful vengeance has just now been exacted in a distant corner of the world." "What vengeance?" says the youth, "and where hath it taken place?" The saint then addressed him thus: "A sulphurous fire hath been poured down from heaven this moment on a city which is subject to Rome, and within the Italian territory, and about three thousand men, besides women and children, have perished. Before the end of this year Gallican sailors shall come here from the provinces of Gaul, and tell thee these same things." His words proved true in a few months; for the same Lugbe, happening to accompany the saint to the Head of the land (Kintyre), inquired at the captain and crew of a bark that had just arrived, and received from them all the news regarding the city and its inhabitants, exactly as it was foretold by the illustrious man.

Chapter 23
The Vision of Saint Columba Concerning Laisran

One very cold day in winter the saint was much afflicted, and wept bitterly. His attendant, Diormit, asked the cause of his sadness, and received this answer from him, "With just reason am I sad today, my little child, seeing that my monks, now wearied after their severe labors, are engaged by Laisran in building a large house; with this I am very much displeased." Strange to say, at that very moment, Laisran, who was living at the time in the monastery of the Oakwood Plain (Derry), felt somehow impelled, and as it were consumed by a fire within him, so that he commanded the monks to stop from working, and some refreshments to be made ready for them. He also gave directions that they were to rest not only that day, but also on other occasions of severe weather. The saint, hearing in spirit these words of consolation addressed by Laisran to his brethren, ceased weeping, and though he himself was living on Iona, he rejoiced with exceeding great joy, and told all the circumstances to his brethren, while at the same time he blessed Laisran for his timely relief to the monks.

Chapter 24
How Feachna the Wise Came as a Penitent to Saint Columba

Another time the saint was sitting on the top of the mountain which overhangs this our monastery, at some distance from it, and turning to his attendant Diormit, said to him, "I am surprised that a certain ship from Ireland does not appear sooner: there is on board a certain wise man who has fallen into a great crime, but who, with tears of repentance, shall soon arrive." Not long after the attendant, looking to the south, saw the sail of a ship that was approaching the harbor. When its arrival was pointed out to the saint he got up quickly and said, "Let us go to meet this stranger, whose sincere penance is accepted by Christ." As soon as Feachna came on shore, he ran to meet the saint, who was coming down to the shore, and falling on his knees before him lamented most bitterly with wailing and tears, and there in the presence of all made open confession of his sins. Then the saint, also shedding tears, said to him, "Arise, my son, and be comforted; the sins thou hast committed are forgiven thee, because, as it is written, 'a humble and contrite heart God doth not despise.'" He then arose, and the saint received him with great joy. After a few days he was sent to Baithene, who at that time was the superior of the monastery in the plain of Lunge (Maigh Lunge, in Tiree), and he journeyed thither in peace.

Chapter 25
The Prophecy of Columba Regarding his Monk Cailtan

At another time he sent two of his monks to another of them named Cailtan, who was then superior in the cell which is called to this day after his brother Dinni, and is situated near the lake of the river Aba (Lochawe). The saint gave them the following instructions, "Run quickly to Cailtan, and tell him to come to me without delay." In obedience to the saint's command they went to the cell of Dinni, and told Cailtan the object of their mission. At once, and without the least delay, he set out along with the messengers of the saint, and soon reached his abode on the Isle of Iona. On making his appearance he was addressed by the saint, "O Cailtan, thou hast done well by coming hither quickly in obedience to my summons; rest now for a while. I sent for you to come to me for this reason, that, loving thee as a friend, I would wish thee to end thy days with me here in true obedience. For before the close of this week thou shalt depart in peace to the Lord." When he heard these words he gave thanks to God, embraced the saint with tears, and receiving his blessing, retired to the guest-chamber. He fell sick that same night, and passed away to Christ the Lord during that very week, as the saint had said.

Chapter 26
The Foresight and Prophecy of the Saint Concerning two Brothers who Were Strangers

One Lord's day a loud cry was heard beyond the above-mentioned Sound of which I speak so often.[16] As soon as the saint heard it, he said to the brethren who were then with him, "Go directly and bring here before us at once the strangers that have now arrived from a distant land." They went accordingly and ferried the strangers across. The saint, after embracing them, asked them at once the object of their journey. In reply they said, "We are come to reside with thee for this year." The saint replied, "With me, as you say, you cannot reside for a year, unless you take first the monastic vow." When those who were present heard these words addressed to strangers who were only newly arrived they wondered very much. But the elder brother, in answer to the saint's remarks, replied, "Although we never up to the present hour entertained the thought before, yet we shall follow your advice, believing that it comes from God." What more need I say? That very moment they entered the chapel with the saint, and on bended knees devoutly took the monastic vow. The saint then turned to his monks and said, "These two strangers who are presenting themselves 'a living sacrifice to God,' and within a short time are fulfilling a long time of Christian warfare, shall pass away in peace this very month to Christ our Lord." The two brothers, on hearing this, gave thanks to God, and were led away to the guest room. After seven days the elder brother fell sick, and departed to the Lord in the course of that week. After other seven days the other brother also fell sick, and within the same week passed to the Lord with joy, so that, according to the truthful prophecy of the saint, both closed their fires in this world within the space of one month.

Chapter 27
The Regarding a Certain Artbranan

When the blessed man was staying for some days on the Isle of Skye, he struck a spot of ground near the sea with his staff, and said to his companions: "Strange to say, my children, this day, an aged heathen, whose natural goodness has been preserved through all his life, will receive baptism, die, and be buried on this very spot." And lo, about an hour after, a boat came into the harbor, on whose prow sat a decrepit old man, the chief of the Geona cohort. Two young men took him out of the boat and laid him at the feet of the blessed man. After being instructed in the word of God by the saint through an interpreter, the old man believed, and was baptized at once by him, and when the baptism was duly administered, he instantly died on the same spot, according to the saint's prediction, and was buried there by his companions, who raised a heap of stones over his grave. This cairn may be seen still on the sea-coast, and the river in which he was baptized is called to this day by the inhabitants, Dobur Artbranan.

Chapter 28
Of the Boat That Was Removed by the Saint's Order

Another time, as the saint was travelling beyond the Dorsal ridge of Britain (Drumalban), he came to a small village, lying amid deserted fields, on the banks of a river, where it flows into a lake. There the saint took up his abode, and that same night, while they were yet but falling asleep, he awoke his companions, and said to them: "Go out this instant with all speed, bring hither quickly the boat you left on the other side of the stream, and put it in a house near us." They did at once as they were ordered, and soon after they were again asleep, the saint roused Diormit, and said to him: "Stand outside the door, and see what has happened to the village in which you had left your boat." Diormit went out accordingly and saw the whole village on fire, and returning to the saint he told him what was taking place. Then the saint told the brethren the name of the rancorous foe who had burnt the houses that night.

Chapter 29
Of Gallan, Son of Fachtna

One day again, as the saint was sitting in his little hut, he said, in prophecy to the same Colca,[17] then reading by his side, "Just now demons are dragging with them down to hell one of the chiefs of thy district who is a niggardly person." When Colca heard this, he marked the time accurately in a tablet, and, coming home within a few months, learned on inquiry from the inhabitants of the place, that Gallan, son of Fachtna, died at the very moment that the saint said to him the man was being carried off by demons.

The Prophecy of the Blessed Man Regarding Findchan, a Priest, and the Founder of the Monastery called in Scotic Artchain, in the Ethican Land (Tiree).

At another time Findchan, the priest and soldier of Christ, named above, brought with him from Scotia (Ireland) to Britain, Aíd, surnamed the Black, descended of a royal family, and a Cruthinian by race.[18] Aíd wore the clerical habit, and came with the purpose of residing with him in the monastery for some years. Now this Aíd the Black had been a very bloodthirsty man, and cruelly murdered many persons, amongst others Diormit, son of Cerbul, by divine appointment king of all. This same Aíd, then, after spending some time in his retirement, was irregularly ordained priest by a bishop invited for the purpose, in the presence of the above-named Findchan. The bishop, however, would not venture to lay a hand upon his head unless Findchan, who was greatly attached to Aíd, in a carnal way, should first place his right hand on his head as a mark of approval. When such an ordination afterwards became known to the saint, he was deeply grieved, and in consequence forthwith pronounced this fearful sentence on the ill-fated Findchan and Aíd: "That right hand which, against the laws of God; and the Church, Findchan placed on the head of the son of perdition, shall soon be covered with sores, and after great and excruciating pain shall precede himself to the grave, and he shall survive the burial of his hand for many years. And Aíd, thus irregularly ordained, shall return as a dog to his vomit, and be again a bloody murderer, until at length, pierced in the neck with a spear, he shall fall from a tree into the water and be drowned."

Such indeed was the end long due to him who murdered the king of all Ireland. The blessed man's prophecy was fulfilled regarding both, for the priest Findchan's right hand festered from the effects of a blow, and went before him into the ground, being buried in an island called Ommon, while he himself survived for many years, according to the saying of St. Columba. But Aíd the Black, a priest only in name, betaking himself again to his former evil doings, and being treacherously wounded with a spear, fell from the prow of a boat into a lake and was drowned.

Of the Consolation Which the Monks, When They Were Weary on Their Journey, Received from the Saint Visiting Them in Spirit

Among these wonderful manifestations of prophetical spirit it does not seem alien from the purpose of our short treatise to mention also here the spiritual comfort which the monks of St. Columba at one time received from his spirit's meeting them by the way. For as the brethren, on one occasion after the harvest work, were returning in the evening to the monastery, and came to a place called in Scotic Cuuleilne, which is said to lie on the western side of Iona island, midway between the field on the plain and our monastery, each of them thought he felt something strange and unusual, which, however, they did not venture to speak of to one another. And so they had the same feeling for some days successively, at the same place, and at the same hour in the evening.

The holy Baithen at that particular time had charge of the work, and one day he said to them: "Now, my brethren, if any of you ever notices anything wonderful and unusual in this spot which lies between the corn-field and the monastery, it is your duty to declare it openly."

An elder brother said, "As you have ordered me, I shall tell you what I observed on this spot. For both in the past few days, and even now, I perceive the fragrance of such a wonderful odor, just as if all the flowers on earth were gathered together into one place; I feel also a glow of heat within me, not at all painful, but most pleasing, and a certain unusual and inexpressible joy poured into my heart, which on a sudden so refreshes and gladdens me, that I forget grief and weariness of every kind. Even the load, however heavy, which I carry on my back, is in some mysterious way so much lightened, from this place all the way to the monastery, which I do not seem to have any weight to bear." What need I add? All the other reapers in turn declared they had exactly the same feeling as the first had described. All then knelt down together, and requested of the holy Baithen that he would learn and inform them of the as yet unknown cause and origin of this wonderful relief, which both he and they were feeling.

"Ye all know," he immediately replied, "our father Columba's tender care regarding us, and how, ever mindful of our toil, he is always grieved when we return later than usual to the monastery. And now because he cannot come in person on this occasion to meet us, his spirit cometh forth to us as we walk along, and conveys to us such great comfort." Having heard these words, they raised their hands to heaven with intense joy as they knelt, and venerated Christ in the holy and blessed man.

I must not pass over another well-authenticated story, told, indeed, by those who heard it, regarding the voice of the blessed man in singing the psalms. The venerable man, when singing in the church with the brethren, raised his voice so wonderfully that it was sometimes heard four furlongs off, that is five hundred paces, and sometimes eight furlongs, that is one thousand paces. But what is stranger still: to those who were with him in the church, his voice did not seem louder than that of others; and yet at the same time persons more than a mile away heard it so distinctly that they could mark each syllable of the verses he was singing, for his voice sounded the same whether far or near. It is however admitted, that this wonderful character in the voice of the blessed man was but rarely observable, and even then it could never happen without the aid of the Holy Ghost.

But another story concerning the great and wonderful power of his voice should not be omitted. The fact is said to have taken place near the fortress of King Brude (near Inverness). When the saint himself was chanting the evening hymns with a few of the brethren, as usual, outside the king's fortifications, some Druids, coming near to them, did all they could to prevent God's praises being sung in the midst of a pagan nation. On seeing this, the saint began to sing the 44th Psalm,[19] and at the same moment so wonderfully loud, like pealing thunder, did his voice become, that king and people were struck with terror and amazement.

Chapter 30
Concerning a Rich Man Named Lugud Clodus

At another time, when the saint was staying some days in Scotia (Ireland), he saw a cleric mounted on a chariot, and driving pleasantly along the plain of Breg (MaghBregh, in Meath). On asking who the person was, the cleric's friend made this reply regarding him: "This is Lugud Clodus, who is rich, and much respected by the people." The saint immediately answered, "He does not seem so to me, but a poor wretched creature, who on the day of his death shall have within his own walled enclosure three of his neighbor's cattle which have strayed on to his property. The best of the strayed cows he shall order to be killed for his own use, and a part of the meat he shall direct to be cooked and served up to him at the very time that he is lying on the same couch with a prostitute, but by the first morsel that he eats shall he be choked and die immediately." Now all these things, as we heard from well-informed persons, afterwards happened according to the saint's prophecy.

Chapter 31
Prophecy of Columba Regarding Neman, Son of Gruthrich

For when the saint corrected this man for his faults, he received the saint's reproof with derision. The blessed man then said to him, "In God's name I will declare these words of truth concerning thee, Neman, that thine enemies shall find thee in bed with a prostitute and put thee to death, and the evil spirits shall carry off thy soul to the place of torments." A few years after his enemies found this same Neman on a couch along with a prostitute in the district of Cainle, and beheaded him, as was foretold by the saint.

Chapter 32
Prophecy of the Holy Man Regarding a Certain Priest

At another time, as the saint was staying in that part of Scotia (Ireland), named a little before,[20] he came by chance on the Lord's day to a neighboring little monastery, called in the Scotic language Trioit (Trevet, in Meath). The same day a priest celebrated the holy mysteries of the Eucharist, who was selected by the brethren who lived there to perform the solemn offices of the Mass, because they thought him very pious. The saint, on hearing him, suddenly opened his mouth and uttered this fearful sentence: "The clean and unclean are now equally mingled together; that is, the clean mysteries of the holy sacrifice are offered by an unclean person, who just now conceals within his own conscience a grievous crime." The bystanders, hearing these words, were struck with terror; but he of whom they were said was forced to confess his sin before them all. And the fellow-soldiers of Christ, who stood round the saint in the church, and had heard him making manifest the secrets of the heart, greatly wondered, and glorified the heavenly knowledge that was seen in him.

Chapter 33
Prophecy Concerning the Robber Erc Mocudruidi

At another time, when the saint was in Iona, he called two of the brothers, Lugbe and Silnan, and gave them this charge, "Sail over now to the Isle of Mull, and on the open ground, near the sea-shore, look for Erc, a robber, who came alone last night in secret from the island Colonsay. He strives to hide himself among the sand hills during the daytime under his boat, which he covers with hay, that he may sail across at night to the little island where our young seals are brought forth and nurtured. When this furious robber has stealthily killed as many as he can, he then fills his boat, and goes back to his hiding-place." They proceeded at once in compliance with their orders, and found the robber lying hid in the very spot that was indicated, and they brought him to the saint, as they had been told. The saint looked at him, and said, "Why do you transgress the commandment of God so often by stealing the property of others? If you are in want at any time, come to us and your needs shall be supplied." At the same time he ordered some wethers to be killed, and given to the wretched thief in place of the seals, that he might not return empty. [21] A short time after the saint saw in spirit that the death of the robber was at hand, and ordered Baithen, then steward in the plain of Lunge (Maigh Lunge, in Tiree), to send a fat sheep and six pecks of corn as a last gift. Baithen sent them at once as the saint had recommended, but he found that the wretched robber had died suddenly the same day, and the presents sent over were used at his burial.

Chapter 34
Prophecy of Regarding the Poet Cronan

At another time, as the saint was sitting one day with the brothers beside the lake Ce (Lough Key, in Roscommon), at the mouth of the river called in Latin Bos (the Boyle), a certain Scotic poet came to them, and when he retired, after a short interview, the brothers said to the saint, "Why did you not ask the poet Cronan, before he went away, to sing us a song with accompaniment, according to the rules of his profession?" The saint replied, "Why do even you now utter such idle words? How could I ask that poor man to sing a song of joy, who has now been murdered, and thus hastily has ended his days, at the hands of his enemies?" The saint had no sooner said these words than immediately a man cried out from beyond the river, "That poet who left you in safety a few minutes ago has just now been met and put to death by his enemies." Then all that were present wondered very much, and looked at one another in amazement.

Chapter 35
Prophecy Regarding the Two Noblemen Who Died

Again, at another time, as the saint was living on Iona, suddenly, while he was reading, and to the great surprise of all, he moaned very heavily. Lugbe Mocublai, who was beside him, on seeing this, asked the cause of such sudden grief. The saint, in very great affliction, answered him, "Two men of royal blood in Scotia have perished of wounds mutually inflicted near the monastery called Cellrois, in the province of the Maugdorna (Maghereoss, in Monaghan); and on the eighth day from the end of this week, one shall give the shout on the other side of the Sound, who has come from Hibernia, and will tell you all as it happened. But oh! My dear child, tell this to nobody so long as I live."

On the eighth day, accordingly, the voice was heard beyond the firth. Then the saint called quietly to Lugbe, and said to him, "This is the aged traveler to whom I alluded, who now cries aloud beyond the strait; go and bring him here to me." The stranger was speedily brought, and told, among other things, how two noblemen in the district of the Maugdorna, near the confines of the territory in which is situate the monastery of Cellrois, died of wounds received in single combat namely, Colman the Hound, son of Ailen, and Ronan, son of Aid, son of Colga, both descended of the kings of the Anteriores (the Airtheara, or people of Oriel in Ulster).

Of His Manner of Receiving Visions

After these things were thus narrated, Lugbe, the soldier of Christ, began to question the saint in private. "Tell me, I entreat of thee, about these and such like prophetic revelations, how they are made to thee, whether by sight or hearing, or other means unknown to man." To this the saint replied, "Thy question regards a most difficult subject, on which I can give thee no information whatever, unless thou first strictly promise, on thy bended knees, by the name of the Most High God, never to communicate this most secret mystery to any person all the days of my life." Hearing this, Lugbe fell at once on his knees, and, with face bent down to the ground, promised everything faithfully as the saint demanded. After this pledge had been promptly given he arose, and the saint said to him, "There are some, though very few, who are enabled by divine grace to see most clearly and distinctly the whole compass of the world, and to embrace within their own wondrously enlarged mental capacity the utmost limits of the heavens and the earth at the same moment, as if all were illumined by a single ray of the sun." In speaking of this miracle, the saint, though he seems to be referring to the experience of other favored persons, yet was in reality alluding to his own, though indirectly, that he might avoid the appearance of vain-glory; and no one can doubt this who reads the apostle Paul, that vessel of election, when he relates the visions revealed to himself. For he did not write, "I know that I," but "I know a man caught up even to the third heavens." Now, although the words seem strictly to refer to another person, yet all admit that he spoke thus of none but himself in his great humility. This was the model followed by our Columba in relating those visions of the Spirit spoken of above, and that, too, in such a way that even Lugbe, for whom the saint showed a special affection, could hardly force him to tell these wonders after much entreaty. And to this fact Lugbe himself, after St. Columba's death, bore witness in the presence of other holy men, from whom I learned the undoubted truths which I have now related of the saint.

Of Cronan the Bishop[22]

At another time, a stranger from the province of the Munstermen, who in his humility did all he could to disguise himself, so that nobody might know he was a bishop, came to the saint; but his rank could not be hidden from the saint. For next Lord's Day, being invited by the saint, as the custom was, to consecrate the Body of Christ, he asked the saint to join him, that, as two priests, they might break the bread of the Lord together. The saint went to the altar accordingly, and suddenly looking into the stranger's face, thus addressed him: "Christ bless thee, brother; do thou break the bread alone, according to the episcopal rite, for I know now that thou art a bishop. Why hast thou disguised thyself so long, and prevented our giving thee the honor we owe to thee?" On hearing the saint's words, the humble stranger was greatly astonished, and adored Christ in His saint, and the bystanders in amazement gave glory to God.

Saint Columba's Prophecy Regarding the Priest Ernan

At another time, the venerable man sent Ernan, his uncle, an aged priest, to preside over the monastery he had founded many years before in Hinba island (Eilean-na-Naoimh). On his departure the saint embraced him affectionately, blessed him, and then foretold what would by and by happen to him, saying,

"This friend of mine, who is now going away from me, I never expect to see alive again in this world." After a few days this same Ernan became very unwell, and desired to be taken back to the saint, who was much rejoiced at his return, and set out for the harbor to meet him. Ernan also himself, though with feeble step, attempted very boldly, and without assistance, to walk from the harbor to meet him; but when there was only the short distance of twenty-four paces between them, death came suddenly upon him before the saint could see his face in life, and he breathed his last as he fell to the ground, that the word of the saint might be fulfilled. Hence on that spot, before the door of the kiln, a cross was raised, and another cross was in like manner put up where the saint resided at the time of his death, which remains unto this day.

Saint Columba's Prophecy Regarding the Family
of a Certain Peasant

At another time, when the saint was staying in that district which is called in the Scotic tongue Coire Salchain (Corrie Sallachan, now Corry, in Morvern), the peasants came to him, and one evening when he saw one of them approaching he said to him, "Where do you live?" "I live," said he, "in that district which borders the shore of Lake Crogreth (Loch Creran)." That district of which you speak," replied the saint, "is now being pillaged by savage marauders." On hearing this, the unhappy peasant began to lament his wife and children; but when the saint saw him so much afflicted he consoled him, saying, "Go, my poor man, go; thy whole family hath escaped by flight to the mountains, but thy cattle, furniture, and other effects the ruthless invaders have taken off with their unjust spoils." When the poor man heard these words he went home, and found that all had happened exactly as the saint foretold.

Prophecy Regarding the Peasant Goire, Son of Aidan

At another time, in the same way, a peasant, who at that time was by far the bravest of all the inhabitants of Korkureti (Corkaree, in Westmeath), asked the saint by what death he would die. "Not in the battle-field shalt thou die," said the saint, "nor at sea; but the travelling companion of whom you have no suspicion shall cause thy death." "Perhaps," said Goire, "one of the friends who accompany me on my journey may be intending to murder me, or my wife, in her love for some younger man, may treacherously kill me?" "Not so," replied the saint. "Why," asked Goire, "wilt thou not tell now the cause of my death?" "Because," said the saint, "I do not wish to tell more clearly just now the companion that is to injure you, lest the frequent thought of the fact should make you too unhappy, until the hour come when you shall find that my words are verified. Why dwell longer on what I have said?" After the lapse of a few years, this same Goire happened to be lying one day under his boat scraping off the bark from a spear-handle, when he heard others fighting near him. He rose hastily to stop the fighting, but his knife, through some neglect in the rapid movement, fell to the ground, and made a very deep wound in his knee. By such a companion, then, was his death caused, and he himself at once remembered with surprise the holy man's prophecy. After a few months he died, carried off by that same wound.

Saint Columba's Foreknowledge and Prophecy Concerning a Matter of Less Moment, but so Beautiful That it Cannot, I Think, be Passed Over in Silence

For at another time, while the saint was living on Iona, he called one of the brothers, and thus addressed him: "In the morning of the third day from this date thou must sit down and wait on the shore on the western side of this island, for a crane, which is a stranger from the northern region of Hibernia, and has been driven about by various winds, shall come, weary and fatigued, after the ninth hour, and lie down before thee on the beach quite exhausted. Treat that bird tenderly, take it to some neighboring house, where it may be kindly received and carefully nursed and fed by thee for three days and three nights. When the crane is refreshed with the three days' rest, and is unwilling to abide any longer with us, it shall fly back with renewed strength to the pleasant part of Scotia (Ireland) from which it originally hath come. This bird do I consign to thee with such special care because it comes from our own native place." The brother obeyed, and on the third day, after the ninth hour, he watched as he was bid for the arrival of the expected guest. As soon as the crane came and alighted on the shore, he took it up gently in its weakness, and carried it to a dwelling that was near, where in its hunger he fed it. On his return to the monastery in the evening, the saint, without any inquiry, but as stating a fact, said to him, "God bless thee, my child, for thy kind attention to this foreign visitor, which shall not remain long on its journey, but return within three days to its old home." As the saint predicted, so exactly did the event prove, for after being nursed carefully for three days, the bird then gently rose on its wings to a great height in the sight of its hospitable entertainer, and marking for a little its path through the air homewards, it directed its course across the sea to Hibernia, straight as it could fly, on a calm day.

The Blessed Man's Foreknowledge Regarding the Battle
Fought Many Years After in the Fortress of Cethirn,
and Regarding the Well Near That Place

Another time, after the convention of the kings at the Ridge of Ceate (Druim Ceatt) that is, of Aidan, son of Gabran, and Aid, son of Ainmure the blessed man returned to the seacoast, and on a calm day in summer he and the Abbot Comgell sat down not far from the above-named fort. Then water was brought in a bronze vessel to the saints from a well that was close by to wash their hands. When St. Columba had received the water, he thus spoke to Abbot Comgell,[23] who was sitting at his side, "A day shall come, O Comgell, when the well whence this water now poured out for us was drawn will be no longer fit for man's use."

"How?" said Comgell, "shall the water of this spring be defiled?"

"From this," said St. Columba, "that it shall be filled with human blood; for thy relatives and mine, that is, the people of the Cruithni and the race of Niall shall be at war in the neighboring fortress of Cethirn (now called the Giant's Sconce, near Coleraine). Whence, at this same well, an unhappy relative of mine shall be slain, and his blood, mingling with that of many others, shall fill it up." This truthful prophecy was duly accomplished after many years, for in that battle, as is well known to many, Domnall, son of Aid, came off victorious, and at that well, according to the saint's word, a near kinsman of his was slain.

Another soldier of Christ, called Finan, who led the life of an anchorite blamelessly for many years near the monastery of the Oakwood Plain (Derry), and who was present at the battle, in relating these things to me, Adomnán, assured me that he saw a man's dead body lying in the well, and that on his return from the battlefield the same day to the monastery of St. Comgell, which is called in the Scotic tongue Cambas (on the river Bann, in diocese of Derry), and from which he had first set out, he found there two aged monks, of St. Comgell, who, when he told them of the battle he saw, and of the well defiled with human blood, at once said to him: "A true prophet is Columba, for he foretold all the circumstances you now mention today regarding the battle and the well, many years indeed before they occurred; this he did in our hearing to St. Comgell, as he sat by the fort Cethirn."

How the Saint was Favored by God's Grace With the
Power of Distinguishing Different Presents

About the same time Conall, bishop of Culerathin (Coleraine) collected almost countless presents from the people of the plain of Eilne (Magh Wine, on the Bann), to give a hospitable reception to the blessed man, and the vast multitude that accompanied him, on his return from the meeting of the kings mentioned above.

Many of these presents from the people were laid out in the paved court of the monastery, that the holy man might bless them on his arrival; and as he was giving the blessing he specially pointed out one present, the gift of a wealthy man. "The mercy of God," said he, "attend the man who gave this, for his charity to the poor and his munificence." Then he pointed out another of the many gifts, and said: "Of this wise and avaricious man's offering, I cannot partake until he repent sincerely of his sin of avarice." Now this saying was quickly circulated among the crowd, and soon reaching the ears of Columb, son of Aid, his conscience reproached him; and he ran immediately to the saint, and on bended knees repented of his sin, promising to forsake his former greedy habits, and to be liberal ever after, with amendment of life. The saint bade him rise: and from that moment he was cured of the fault of greediness, for he was truly a wise man, as was revealed to the saint through that present.

But the munificent rich man, called Brenden, of whose present mention was made above, hearing the words of the saint regarding himself, knelt down at his feet and besought him to pray for him to the Lord. When at the outset the saint reproved him for certain other sins of which he was guilty, he expressed his heartfelt sorrow, and purpose of amendment. And thus both these men were cured of the peculiar vices in which they were wont to indulge. With like knowledge at another time, on the occasion of his visit to the Great Cell of Deathrib (Kilmore, in Roscommon), the saint knew the offering of a stingy man, called Diormit, from many others collected in that place on his arrival.

To have written thus much in the course of this first Book selecting a few instances out of many of the prophetic gifts of the blessed man, may suffice. Indeed, I have recorded only a few facts regarding this venerable person, for no doubt there were very many more which could not come to men's knowledge, from being hidden under a kind of sacramental character while those mentioned were like a few little drops which oozed out, as it were, like newly fermented wine through the chinks of a full vessel. For holy and apostolic men, in general, in order to avoid vain-glory, strive as much as they can to conceal the wonders of God's secret working within them. Yet God sometimes, whether they will or no, makes some of these known to the world, and brings them into view by various means, wishing thus, as He does, to honor those saints who honor Him, that is, our Lord Himself, to whom be glory forever, and ever.

Here ends this first Book, and the next Book treats of the wonderful miracles, which generally accompanied his prophetic foreknowledge.

Book One Notes

1 Iona
2 Scotland
3 King Bridei I, r. 554-584.
4 Probably Finnian of Movilla or Finnian of Clonard.
5 The famous Caedwalla of Bede. The reference is to the Battle of Hatfield Chase in October of 633, fought 36 years after St. Columba's death.
6 High-kings of Anglo-Saxon England. Tradition counts seven: Ælle of Sussex, Caewlin of Wessex, Ethelbert of Kent, Raedwald of East Anglia, Edwin of Deira, Oswald of Northumbria, and Oswy of Northumbria.
7 Irish.

8 St. Fintán of Taghmon, d. 635.

9 Daire Calgaich, or Derry

10 Iona

11 St. Cainnech or Canice, also known as St. Kenneth in Scotland. Cainnech (516-600), one of the Twelve Apostles of Ireland, arrived in Iona in the year 565 to aid St. Columba in the evangelization of the Picts. He later went on to found the famed St. Andrews in Scotland.

12 These "deserts" were solitary islands where the monks could live in solitude: "The other form of this solitary life was one in which inmate of a monastery withdrew from the world altogether and sought out some remote and desert spot or island in which he might pass the rest of his life in total solitude. Such retreats were called emphatically 'Deserts'. Of this desire which with many became almost a passion Adomnán gives us an instance in Cormac ua Leathan" (*Celtic Scotland: Church and Culture*. William Forbes Skene. Edmonson & Douglas, 1877, p. 247).

13 King Áedán mac Gabráin of Dál Riata, also called Áedán the Wily or the Treacherous (r. 574-609). An important figure in his time, King Áedán is referenced in the histories of the Irish, Picts, Anglo-Saxons and even the Welsh. He was eventually defeated and deposed by the Anglo-Saxon Æthelfrith of Berenicia. He appears to have enjoyed the support of St. Columba.

14 See Chapter 6, note 12 above.

15 It the Celtic countries it was common for penitents to retreat to islands specially designated as places of penance.

16 The Sound of Iona.

17 See Book I, Chapters 10 & 11.

18 Cruthinian: Southern Antrim in northeast Ireland.

19 Psalm 45 in the modern numbering.

20 The Plains of Breg in County Meath.

21 Wether: A male sheep castrated before the age of sexual maturity

22 Neither the famous St. Crónán of Mochua, nor St. Crónán of Roscrea, both of whom lived too late to have known St. Columba, but another bishop by this name.

23 The great St. Comall of Bangor, friend of St. Columba and associate of great saints such as St. Brendan, St. Cormac, and St. Finnian of Moville.

Book Two
On His Miraculous Powers

Chapter 1
Of the Water Which was Turned to Wine

At another time, while the venerable man was yet a youth in Ireland learning the wisdom of the Holy Scripture under St. Findbarr, the bishop, it happened that on a festival day not the least drop of wine could be found for the mystic sacrifice. Hearing the ministers of the altar complaining among themselves of this want, he took the vessel and went to the fountain, that, as a deacon, he might bring pure spring water for the celebration of the Holy Eucharist; for at that time he was himself serving in the order of deacon. The holy man then blessed in faith that element of water taken from the spring, invoking, as he did so, the name of our Lord Jesus Christ, who in Cana of Galilee had changed water into wine: and the result was that by His operation in this miracle also, an inferior element, namely pure water, was changed into one of a more excellent kind, namely wine, by the hands of this illustrious man. The holy man, then returning from the fountain and entering the church, placed beside the altar the vessel containing this liquid, and said to the ministers: "Here is wine, which the Lord Jesus hath sent, for the celebration of His mysteries." The holy bishop and his ministers, having ascertained the fact, returned most ardent thanks to God. But the holy youth ascribed this, not to himself, but to the holy bishop Vinnian. This first proof of miraculous power, Christ the Lord manifested in His disciple, just as under like circumstances He had made it the first of His own miracles in Cana of Galilee.

Let this divine miracle, worked by our Columba, shine as a light in the beginning of this book, that it may lead us on to the other divine and miraculous powers which were seen in him.[1]

Chapter 2
Of the Bitter Fruit of a Tree Changed Sweet

There was a certain very fruitful apple tree on the south side of the monastery of the Oakwood Plain (Derry), in its immediate vicinity. When the inhabitants of the place were complaining of the exceeding bitterness of the fruit, the saint one day in autumn, came to it, and seeing the boughs bearing to no purpose a load of fruit that injured rather than pleased those who tasted it, he raised his holy hand and blessed it, saying, "In the name of the Almighty God, O bitter tree, let all thy bitterness depart from thee; and let all thy apples, hitherto so very bitter, be now changed into the sweetest." Wonderful to behold, quicker than the word, and at that very instant, all the apples of the tree lost their bitterness, and were changed to an amazing sweetness, according to the saint's word.

Chapter 3
Of Corn Sown After Midsummer

At another time the saint sent his monks to bring from the little farm of a peasant some bundles of twigs to build a dwelling. When they returned to the saint, with a freight-ship laden with the foresaid bundles of twigs, they told the saint that the poor man was very sorry on account of the loss. The saint immediately gave them these directions, saying, "Lest we do the man any wrong, take to him from us twice three measures of barley, and let him sow it now in his arable land." According to the saint's orders, the corn was sent and delivered over to the poor man, who was called Findchan, with the above directions.

He received them with thanks, but asked, "What good can any corn do, which is sown after midsummer, against the nature of this soil?"

But his wife, on the contrary, said, "Do what you have been ordered by the saint, to whom the Lord will give whatever he asks from Him." And the messengers likewise said further, "St. Columba, who sent us to you with this gift, entrusted us also with this form of instruction regarding your crop, saying, 'Let that man trust in the omnipotence of God; his corn, though sown now, when twelve days of the month of June are passed, shall be reaped in the beginning of the month of August.'"

The peasant accordingly ploughed and sowed, and the crop which, against hope, he sowed at the above-mentioned time he gathered in ripe, to the admiration of all his neighbors, in the beginning of the month of August, in that place which is [now] called Delcros.

Chapter 4
Of a Cloud of Pestilence and the Curing of Many

At another time also, while the saint was living on Iona and was sitting on the little hill which is called, in Latin, Munitio Magna,[2] he saw in the north a dense rainy cloud rising from the sea on a clear day. As the saint saw it rising, he said to one of his monks, named Silnan, son of Nemandon Mocusogin, who was sitting beside him, "This cloud will be very baleful to man and beast, and after rapidly passing today over a considerable part of Scotia (Ireland) namely, from the stream called Ailbine (Delvin, in Meath) as far as the Ford Clied (Athcliath, now Dublin) it will discharge in the evening a pestilential rain, which will raise large and putrid ulcers on the bodies of men and on the udders of cows; so that men and cattle shall sicken and die, worn out with that poisonous complaint. But we, in pity for their sufferings, ought to relieve them by the merciful aid of God; do thou therefore, Silnan, come down with me from this hill, and prepare for thy tomorrow's voyage. If God be willing and life spared to us, you shall receive from me some bread which has been blessed by the invocation of the name of God; this thou shalt dip in water, and on thy sprinkling therewith man and beast, they shall speedily recover their health." Why need we linger over it? On the next day, when all things necessary had been hastily got ready, Silnan received the blessed bread from the hands of the saint, and set out on his voyage in peace. As he was starting, the saint gave him these words of comfort, saying, "Be of good courage, my dear son, for thou shalt have fair and pleasant breezes day and night till thou come to that district which is called Ard-Ceannachta (in Meath), that you may bring the more speedily relief with the healing bread to those who are there sick." What more? Silnan, obeying the saint's words, had a quick and prosperous voyage, by the aid of God, and coming to the above-mentioned part of the district, found the people of whom the saint had been speaking destroyed by the pestilential rain falling down from the aforesaid cloud, which had passed rapidly on before him. In the first place, twice three men were found in the same house near the sea reduced to the agonies of approaching death, and when they were sprinkled by Silnan with the blessed water, were very happily healed that very day.

The report of this sudden cure was soon carried through the whole country which was attacked by this most fatal disease, and drew all the sick people to St. Columba's messenger, who, according to the saint's orders, sprinkled man and beast with the water in which the blessed bread had been dipped, and immediately they were restored to perfect health; then the people finding themselves and their cattle healed, praised with the utmost expression of thankfulness Christ in St. Columba.

Now, in the incidents here related these two things, I think, are clearly associated—namely, the gift of prophecy regarding the cloud and the miraculous power in healing the sick. And to the truth of all these things, in every particular, the above-named Silnan, the soldier of Christ and messenger of St. Columba, bore testimony in the presence of the Abbot Segine and the other fathers.

Chapter 5
Of Maugina the Holy Virgin

At another time, while the saint was staying on Iona, he one day at prime called to him a certain brother, named Lugaid, who in the Scotic tongue was surnamed Lathir, and thus addressed him, saying, "Prepare quickly for a rapid voyage to Scotia (Ireland), for it is of the very utmost importance to me that thou be sent with a message from me to Clocher, of the sons of Daimen (Clogher). For this last night, by some accident, the holy virgin Maugina, daughter of Daimen, when she was returning home from the oratory after mass, stumbled and broke her thigh quite through. She is now crying out, and very often calling on my name, in hope that through me she may receive some comfort from the Lord." What more need I say? As Lugaid was setting out in accordance with the directions given him, the saint gave him a little box made of pine, saying, "Let the blessed gift which is contained in this little box be dipped in a vessel of water when you come to visit Maugina, and let the water thus blessed be poured on her thigh; then at once, by the invocation of God's name, her thigh-bone shall be joined together and made strong, and the holy virgin shall recover perfect health.' This, too, the saint added, "Lo! Here in thy presence I write on the lid of this little box the number of twenty-three years, which the holy virgin shall enjoy of this present life after receiving her health."

All this was exactly fulfilled as the saint had foretold; for as soon as Lugaid came to the holy virgin her thigh was washed, as the saint recommended, with the blessed water, and was in an instant completely healed by the closing up of the bone. At the arrival of the messenger of St. Columba, she expressed her joy in the most earnest thanksgiving, and, after recovering her health, she lived, according to the prophecy of the saint, twenty-three years in the constant practice of good works.

Chapter 6
Of the Cures of Diseases in the Ridge of Ceate

We have been told by well-informed persons that this man of admirable life, by invoking the name of Christ, healed the disorders of various sick persons in the course of that short time which he spent at the Ridge of Ceate, when attending there the meeting of the kings. For either by his merely stretching out his holy hand, or by the sprinkling of the sick with the water blessed by him, or by their touching even the hem of his cloak, or by their receiving his blessing on anything, as, for instance, on bread or salt, and dipping it in water, they who believed recovered perfect health.

Chapter 7
Of a Lump of Salt Blessed by the Saint

On another occasion also, Colga, son of Cellach, asked and obtained from the saint a lump of salt which he had blessed, for the cure of his sister, who had nursed him, and was now suffering from a very severe attack of ophthalmia. This same sister and nurse having received such a blessed gift from the hand of her brother, hung it up on the wall over her bed; and after some days it happened by accident that a destructive fire entirely consumed the village where this took place, and with others the house of the aforesaid woman. Yet, strange to say, in order that the gift of the blessed man might not be destroyed, the portion of the wall from which it was suspended still stood uninjured after the rest of the house had been burned down; nor did the fire venture to touch even the two uprights from which the lump of salt was suspended.

Chapter 8
Of a Book in the Saint's Handwriting Which Could Not be Destroyed by Water

I cannot think of leaving unnoticed another miracle which once took place by means of the opposite element. For many years after the holy man had departed to the Lord, a certain youth fell from his horse into the river which in Scotic is called Boend (the Boyne), and, being drowned, was for twenty days under the water. When he fell he had a number of books packed up in a leathern satchel under his arm; and so, when he was found after the above-mentioned number of days, he still had the satchel of books pressed between his arm and side. When the body was brought out to the dry ground, and the satchel opened, it was found to contain, among the volumes of other books, which were not only injured, but even rotten, a volume written by the sacred fingers of St. Columba; and it was as dry and wholly uninjured as if it had been enclosed in a desk.

Of Another Miracle in Similar Circumstances

At another time a book of hymns for the office of every day in the week, and in the handwriting of St. Columba, having slipped, with the leathern satchel which contained it, from the shoulder of a boy who fell from a bridge, was immersed in a certain river in the province of the Lagenians (Leinster). This very book lay in the water from the Feast of the Nativity of our Lord till the end of the Paschal season, and was afterwards found on the bank of the river by some women who were walking there: it was brought by them in the same satchel, which was not only soaked, but even rotten, to a certain priest named Iogenan, a Pict by race, to whom it formerly belonged. On opening the satchel himself, Iogenan found his book uninjured, and as clean and dry as if it had been as long a time in his desk, and had never fallen into the water. And we have ascertained, as undoubted truth, from those who were well informed in the matter; that the like things happened in several places with regard to books written by the hands of St. Columba namely, that the books could suffer no injury from being immersed in water. But the account we have given of the above-mentioned book of Iogenan we have received from certain truthful, excellent, and honorable men, who saw the book itself, perfectly white and beautiful, after a submersion of so many days, as we have stated.

These two miracles, though wrought in matters of small moment, and shown in opposite elements namely, fire and water, redound to the honor of the blessed man, and prove his great and singular merits before the Lord.

Chapter 9
Of Water Drawn From the Rock by the Saint's Prayers

And since mention has been made a little before of the element of water, we must not pass over in silence some other miracles which the Lord wrought by the saint at different times and places, in which the same element was concerned. On another occasion, then, when the saint was engaged in one of his journeys, a child was presented to him in the course of his travels for baptism by its parents; and because there was no water to be found in the neighborhood, the saint turned aside to a rock that was near, and kneeling down prayed for a short time; then rising up after his prayer, he blessed the face of the rock, from which there immediately gushed out an abundant stream of water; and there he forthwith baptized the child.

Concerning the child that was baptized he uttered the following prophecy, saying, "This child shall live to a very great age; in his youth he will indulge freely the desires of the flesh; afterwards he will devote himself to the warfare of a Christian until the very end of his life, and thus depart to the Lord in a good old age." All this happened to the man according to the prophecy of the saint. This was Lugucencalad, whose parents were from [the region of] Artdaib Muirchol (Ardnamurchan), where there is seen even to this day a well called by the name of St. Columba.

Chapter 10
Of a Poisonous Fountain of Water Made Sweet

Again, while the blessed man was stopping for some days in the province of the Picts, he heard that there was a fountain famous amongst this heathen people, which foolish men, having their senses blinded by the devil, worshipped as a god. For those who drank of this fountain, or purposely washed their hands or feet in it, were allowed by God to be struck by demoniacal art, and went home either leprous or purblind, or at least suffering from weakness or other kinds of infirmity. By all these things the Pagans were seduced, and paid divine honour to the fountain. Having ascertained this, the saint one day went up to the fountain fearlessly; and, on seeing this, the Druids, whom he had often sent away from him vanquished and confounded, were greatly rejoiced, thinking that he would suffer like others from the touch of that baneful water. But he, having first raised his holy hand and invoked the name of Christ, washed his hands and feet; and then with his companions, drank of the water which he had blessed. And from that day the demons departed from the fountain; and not only was it not allowed to injure any one, but even many diseases amongst the people were cured by this same fountain, after it had been blessed and washed in by the saint.

Chapter 11
Of the Danger to the Blessed Man at Sea and the Sudden Calm Produced by His Prayers

At another time the holy man began to be in great danger at sea, for the whole vessel was violently tossed and shaken with the huge dashing waves, and a great storm of wind was raging on all hands. The sailors then chanced to say to the saint, as he was trying to help them to bale the vessel, "What thou art now doing is of little use to us in our present danger, thou shouldst rather pray for us as we are perishing." On hearing this he ceased to throw out the bitter waters of the green sea wave, and began to pour out a sweet and fervent prayer to the Lord. Wonderful to relate! The very moment the saint stood up at the prow, with his hands stretched out to heaven and prayed to the Almighty, the whole storm of wind and the fury of the sea ceased more quickly than can be told, and a perfect calm instantly ensued. But those who were in the vessel were amazed, and giving thanks with great admiration, glorified the Lord in the holy and illustrious man.

Chapter 12
Of Another Similar Peril at Sea

At another time, also, when a wild and dangerous storm was raging, and his companions were crying out to the saint to pray to the Lord for them, he gave them this answer, saying, "On this day it is not for me, but for that holy man, the Abbot Cainnech, to pray for you in your present peril." What I am to relate is wonderful. The very same hour St. Cainnech[3] was in his monastery, which in Latin is called Campulus Bovis, but in Scotic

Ached-bou (Aghaboe, in Queen's County), and heard with the inner ear of his heart, by a revelation of the Holy Ghost, the aforesaid words of St. Columba; and when he had just begun to break the blessed bread in the refectory after the ninth hour, he hastily left the table, and with one shoe on his foot, while the other in his extreme haste was left behind, he went quickly to the church, saying, "It is not for us now to take time to dine, when the vessel of St. Columba is in danger at sea, for at this moment he is lamenting, and calling on the name of Cainnech to pray to Christ for him and his companions in peril." When he had said this he entered the oratory and prayed for a short time on his bended knees; and the Lord heard his prayer, the storm immediately ceased, and the sea became very calm. Whereupon St. Columba, seeing in spirit, though there was a far distance between them, the haste of Cainnech in going to the church, uttered, to the wonder of all, from his pure heart, these words, saying, "Now I know, O Cainnech, that God has heard thy prayer; now hath thy swift running to the church with a single shoe greatly profited us." In such a miracle as this, then, we believe that the prayers of both saints had their share in the work.

Chapter 13
Of the Staff of Saint Cainnech

On another occasion, the same Cainnech above mentioned embarked for Scotia (Ireland) from the harbor of Iona, and forgot to take his staff with him. After his departure the staff was found on the shore, and given into the hands of St. Columba, who, on his return home, brought it into the oratory, and remained there for a very long time alone in prayer. Cainnech, meanwhile, on approaching the Oidechan island (Oidech, near Isla) suddenly felt pricked at heart at the thought of his forgetfulness, and was deeply afflicted at it. But after some time, leaving the vessel, and falling upon his knees in prayer on the ground, he found before him on the turf of the little land of Aithche the staff which, in his forgetfulness, he had left behind him at the landing-place in Iona. He was greatly surprised at its being thus brought to him by the divine power, and gave thanks to God.

Chapter 14
Of the Favorable Wind Obtained by Baithene and Columban Through the Prayers of the Blessed Man

At another time, also, the above-named holy men came in company to the saint, and asked him, with one consent, to seek and obtain for them from the Lord a favorable wind on the next day, though they were to set out in different directions. The saint in answer gave them this reply, "To-morrow morning, Baithene, setting sail from the harbor of Iona, shall have a favorable wind until he reaches the landing-place of the plain of Lunge." And the Lord granted this favor according to the word of the saint; for Baithene on that same day crossed, with full sails, the whole of the open sea, as far as the Ethican land (Tiree). But at the third hour of the same day, the venerable man called to him the priest Columban, saying, "Baithene has now happily arrived at the wished-for haven, prepare thou then to sail to-day; the Lord will soon change the wind to the north." And the same hour the wind from the south obeying the word thus spoken by the holy man, wheeled round and became a northern breeze; and thus on the same day these two holy men departed the one from the other in peace and both set sail, Baithene in the morning for the Ethican land (Tiree), and Columban in the afternoon for Hibernia, and made the voyages with full sails and fair winds. The Lord wrought this miracle in answer to the prayer of the illustrious man, according as it is written, "All things are possible to him that believeth." After the departure of St. Columban on that day, St. Columba uttered this prophecy concerning him: "The holy man, Columban, whom we have blessed on his departure, shall never see my face again in this world." And this was afterwards fulfilled, for the same year St. Columban passed away to the Lord.[4]

Chapter 15
Of the Driving out of a Demon that Lurked in a Milk Pail

At another time, a certain youth, named Columban, grandson of Brian, came forward hurriedly, and stopped at the door of the little cell in which the blessed man was writing. This same person, being on his way home from the milking of the cows, and carrying on his back a vessel full of new milk, asked the saint to bless his burden, as he usually did. Then the saint, being at the time at some distance away in front of him, raised his hand, and formed the saving sign in the air, which at once was greatly agitated; the bar, which fastened the lid of the pail, being pushed back through the two openings that received it, was shot away to a great distance, while the lid fell to the earth, and the greater part of the milk was spilled upon the ground. The young lad then laid down the vessel, with the little milk that remained, on its bottom on the ground, and kneeled down in prayer. The saint said to him, "Rise up, Columban, for thou hast acted negligently in thy work today, inasmuch as thou didst not banish the demon that lurked in the bottom of the empty vessel by forming on it the sign of the cross of our Lord before the milk was poured into it; and now, as thou seest, being unable to bear the power of that sign, he has quickly fled in terror, troubled the whole vessel in every corner, and spilled the milk. Bring the vessel, then, nearer to me here that I may bless it." This being done, the half-empty pail, which the saint had blessed, was found the same instant, filled by divine agency; and the little that had previously remained in the bottom was at once increased under the blessing of his holy hand, so as to fill it to the brim.

Chapter 16
Concerning a Vessel Which a Sorcerer Named Silnan
had Filled With Milk Taken From a Bull

The following is told as having occurred in the house of a rich peasant named Foirtgirn, who lived in Mount Cainle. When the saint was staying there, he decided justly a dispute between two rustics, whose coming to him he knew beforehand: and one of them, who was a sorcerer, took milk, by his diabolical art, at the command of the saint, from a bull that was near. This the saint directed to be done, not to confirm these sorceries—God forbid!—but to put an end to them in the presence of all the people. The blessed man, therefore, demanded that the vessel, full, as it seemed to be, of this milk, should be immediately given to him; and he blessed it with this sentence, saying: "Now it shall in this way be proved that this is not true milk, as it is supposed to be, but blood, which is colored by the artifice of demons to impose on men." This was no sooner said than the milky color gave place to the true natural color of blood. The bull also, which in the space of one hour wasted and pined away with a hideous leanness, and was all but dead, was sprinkled with water that had been blessed by the saint, and recovered with astonishing rapidity.

Chapter 17
Of Lugne Mocumin

One day a young man of good disposition and parts, named Lugne, who afterwards, in his old age, was prior of the monastery of the Elena island (Eileen Naomh, now Nave island, near Isla), came to the saint, and complained of a bleeding which for many months had often poured profusely from the nostrils. Having asked him to come nearer, the saint pressed both his nostrils with two fingers of his right hand and blessed him. And from that hour when he received the blessing, till the last day of his life, a drop of blood never came from his nose.

Chapter 18
Of the Fishes Provided by God for the Blessed Man

On another occasion, when some hardy fishermen, companions of this renowned man, had taken five fish in their net in the river Sale (the Shiel, or Seil), which abounds in fish, the saint said to them, "Try again," said he; "cast thy net into the stream, and you shall at once find a large fish which the Lord has provided for me." In obedience to the saint's command they hauled in their nets a salmon of astonishing size, which God had provided for him.

Chapter 19
Of the River Salmon Provided by God for Columba

At another time also, when the saint was stopping some, days beside the lake of Ce (Loughkey, in Roscommon), he delayed his companions when they were anxious to go a-fishing, saying: "No fish will be found in the river today or to-morrow; but on the third day I will send you, and you shall find two large river-salmon taken in the net." And so, after two short days, they cast their nets, and landed two, of the most extraordinary size, which they found in the river which is named Boyle. In the capture of fish on these two occasions, the power of miracles appears accompanied at the same time by a prophetic foreknowledge, and for both graces the saint and his companions gave fervent thanks to God.

Chapter 20
*Regarding Nesan the Crooked, Who Lived
in the Country Bordering on Lochaber*

This Nesan, though very poor, joyfully received on one occasion the saint as his guest. And after he had entertained him as hospitably as his means would afford for one night, the saint asked him the number of his heifers. He answered, "Five." The saint then said, "Bring them to me that I may bless them." And when they were brought the saint raised his holy hand and blessed them, and said: "From this day thy five little heifers shall increase to the number of one hundred and five cows." And as this same Nesan was a man of humble condition, having a wife and children, the saint added this further blessing, saying: "Thy seed shall be blessed in thy children and grandchildren." And all this was completely fulfilled without any failure, according to the word of the saint.

Chapter 21
On Uigene the Stingy

On the other hand, he pronounced the following prophetic sentence on a certain rich and very stingy man named Uigene, who despised St. Columba, and showed him no hospitality, saying: "But the riches of that niggardly man who hath despised Christ in the strangers that came to be his guests, will gradually become less from this day, and be reduced to nothing; and he himself shall be a beggar; and his son shall go about from house to house with a half-empty wallet: and he shall be slain by a rival beggar with an axe, in the pit of a threshing floor." All this was exactly fulfilled in both cases, according to the prophecy of the holy man.

Chapter 22
How the Holy Man Blessed the Few Cattle Belonging to Columban,
a Man of Equally Humble Condition; and How, After his Blessing,
They Increased to the Number of a Hundred

At another time also, the blessed man was one night kindly treated as his guest by the aforesaid Columban, who was then very poor, and, as he had done before in the above account of Nesan, he asked his host, early next morning, as to the amount and kind of his goods. When asked, he said: "I have only five small cows, but if thou bless them they will increase to more." And immediately he was directed by the saint to bring them before him, and in the same manner as was related concerning the five cows of Nesan, he gave as rich a blessing to those of Columban, and said, "You shalt have, by God's gift, a hundred and five cows, and an abundant blessing shall be also upon thy children and grandchildren." All this was granted to the full in his lands, and cattle, and offspring, according to the prophecy of the blessed man; and, what is very strange, the number of cattle determined by the saint for both these men, whenever it reached one hundred and five, could not in any way be increased; for those that were beyond this stated number, being carried off by various accidents, never appeared to be of any value, except in so far as anything might be employed for the use of the family, or spent in almsgiving. In this history, then, as in the others, the gifts both of miracles and prophecy are clearly shown together, for in the large increase of the cattle we see the virtue of his blessing and of his prayer, and, in the determination of the number, his prophetic knowledge.

Chapter 23
Of the Death of Some Wicked Men

The venerable man had a great love for the above-named Columban, on account of the many acts of kindness he had done to him, and caused him by blessing him, from being poor to become very rich. Now, there was at that time a certain wicked man, a persecutor of the good, named Joan, son of Conall, son of Domnall, sprung from the royal tribe of Gabran. This man troubled the foresaid Columban, the friend of St. Columba; and not once, but twice, attacked and plundered his house and carried off all he could find in it. Hence it not unfitly happened to this wicked man, that as he and his associates, after having plundered the house of the same person a third time, were returning to their vessel, laden with plunder, he met advancing towards him, the holy man whom he had despised, when he thought he was afar off. When the saint reproached him for his evil deeds, and advised and besought him to give up the plunder, he remained hardened and obstinate, and scorned the holy man; and thus mocking and laughing at the blessed man, he embarked with the booty. Yet the saint followed him to the water's edge, and wading up to the knees in the clear green sea-water, with both his hands raised to heaven, earnestly invoked Christ, who glorifies His elect, who are giving glory to Him.

Now the haven where he thus for some time stood and besought the Lord after the departure of the oppressor, is at a place called in Scotic Ait-Chambas Art-Muirchol (Camus-an-Gaall, Ardnamurchan). Then the saint, as soon as he had finished his prayer, returned to the dry ground, and sat down on the higher ground with his companions, and spoke to them in that hour these very terrible words, saying: "This miserable wretch who, hath despised Christ in His servants will never return to the port from which you have now seen him set sail: neither shall he, nor his wicked associates, reach the land for which they are bound, for a sudden death shall prevent it. This day a furious storm shall proceed from a cloud, which you will soon see rising in the north, shall overwhelm him and his companions, so that not one of them will survive to tell the tale."

After the lapse of a few moments, even while the day was perfectly calm, behold! A cloud arose from the sea, as the saint had said, and caused a great hurricane, which overtook the plunderer with his spoil, between the Malean and Colosus islands (Mull and Colonsay), and overwhelmed him in the midst of the sea, which was suddenly lashed into fury: and not even one of those in the vessel escaped, as the saint had said: and in this wonderful manner, by such a singular storm, while the whole sea around remained quiet, were the robbers miserably, but justly, overwhelmed and sunk into the deep.

Chapter 24
Of a Certain Feradach, Cut Off by Sudden Death

At another time also, the holy man specially recommended a certain exile, of noble race among the Picts, named Tarain, to the care of one Feradach, a rich man, who lived in the Ilean island (Isla), that he might be received in his retinue for some months as one of his friends. After he had accepted the person thus highly recommended at the hand of the holy man, he in a few days acted treacherously, and cruelly ordered him to be put to death. When the news of this horrid crime was carried by travelers to the saint, he replied by the following prediction: "That unhappy wretch hath not lied unto me, but unto God, and his name shall be blotted out of the book of life. We are speaking these words now in the middle of summer, but in autumn, before he shall eat of swine's flesh that hath been fattened on the fruits of the trees, he shall be seized by a sudden death, and carried off to the infernal regions."

When the miserable man was told this prophecy of the saint, he scorned and laughed at him; and when some days of the autumn months had passed, he ordered a sow that had been fattened on the kernels of nuts to be killed, none of his other swine having yet been slaughtered: he ordered also, that its entrails should be immediately taken out and a piece quickly roasted for him on the spit, so that by hurrying and eating of it thus early, he might falsify the prediction of the blessed man. As soon as it was roasted he asked for a very small morsel to taste it, but before the hand which he stretched out to take it had reached his mouth he expired, and fell down on his back a corpse. And all who saw or heard it were greatly astonished and terrified; and they honored and glorified Christ in his holy prophet.

Chapter 25
Concerning a Certain Other Impious Man, a Persecutor of the Churches, Called in Latin Manus Dextera

On one occasion when the blessed man was living in the Hinba island (Eilean-na-Naoimh), and set about excommunicating some destroyers of the churches, and amongst them the sons of Conall, son of Domnall, one of whom was the Joan before mentioned,[5] one of their wicked associates was instigated by the devil to rush on the saint with a spear, on purpose to kill him. To prevent this, one of the brethren, named Findlugan, put on the saint's cowl and interposed, being ready to die for the holy man. But in a wonderful way the saint's garment served as a kind of strong and impenetrable fence which could not be pierced by the thrust of a very sharp spear though made by a powerful man, but remained untouched, and he who had it on was safe and uninjured under the protection of such a guard. But the ruffian who did this, whose name was Manus Dextera,[6] retraced his steps thinking he had transfixed the saint with his spear. Exactly a year afterwards, when the saint was staying in Iona, he said, "A year is just now elapsed since the day Manus Dextera did what he could to put Findlugan to death in my place; but he himself is slain, I believe, this very hour." And so it happened, at that very moment, according to the revelation of the saint, in the island which in Latin may be called Longa (Luing), where, in a battle fought between a number of men on both sides, this Manus Dextera alone was slain by Cronan, son of Baithene, with a dart, shot, it is said, in the name of St. Columba; and when he fell the battle ceased.

Chapter 26
Of yet Another Oppressor of the Innocent

When the holy man, while yet a youth in deacon's orders, was living in the region of Leinster, learning the divine wisdom, it happened one day that an unfeeling and pitiless oppressor of the innocent was pursuing a young girl who fled before him on a level plain. As she chanced to observe the aged Gemman, master of the foresaid young deacon, reading on the plain, she ran straight to him as fast as she could. Being alarmed at such an unexpected occurrence, he called on Columba, who was reading at some distance, that both together, to the best of their ability, might defend the girl from her pursuer; but he immediately came up, and without any regard to their presence, stabbed the girl with his lance under their very cloaks, and leaving her lying dead at their feet turned to go away back. Then the old man, in great affliction, turning to Columba, said: "How long, holy youth Columba, shall God, the just Judge, allow this horrid crime and this insult to us to go unpunished?" Then the saint at once pronounced this sentence on the perpetrator of the deed: "At the very instant the soul of this girl whom he has murdered ascends into heaven, so shall the soul of the murderer go down into hell." And scarcely had he spoken the words when the murderer of the innocent, like Ananias before Peter, fell down dead on the spot before the eyes of the holy youth. The news of this sudden and terrible vengeance was soon spread abroad throughout many districts of Scotia (Ireland), and with it the wonderful fame of the holy deacon.

What we have said may suffice concerning the terrible punishments inflicted on those who were opposed to him; we will now relate a few things regarding wild beasts.

Chapter 27
How a Wild Boar Was Destroyed Through his Prayers

On one occasion when the blessed man was staying some days in the Island of Skye, he left the brethren and went alone a little farther than usual to pray; and having entered a dense forest he met a huge wild boar that happened to be pursued by hounds. As soon as the saint saw him at some distance, he stood looking intently at him. Then raising his holy hand and invoking the name of God in fervent prayer, he said to it, "Thou shalt proceed no further in this direction: perish in the spot which thou hast now reached." At the sound of these words of the saint in the woods, the terrible brute was not only unable to proceed farther, but by the efficacy of his word immediately fell dead before his face.

Chapter 28[7]
How an Aquatic Monster Was Driven Off by Virtue of the Blessed Man's Prayer

On another occasion also, when the blessed man was living for some days in the province of the Picts, he was obliged to cross the river Ness; and when he reached the bank of the river, he saw some of the inhabitants burying an unfortunate man, who, according to the account of those who were burying him, was a short time before seized, as he was swimming, and bitten most severely by a monster that lived in the water; his wretched body was, though too late, taken out with a hook, by those who came to his assistance in a boat. The blessed man, on hearing this, was so far from being dismayed, that he directed one of his companions [Lugne Mocumin] to swim over and row across the coble that was moored at the farther bank. And Lugne Mocumin hearing the command of the excellent man, obeyed without the least delay, taking off all his clothes, except his tunic, and leaping into the water. But the monster, which, so far from being satiated, was only roused for more prey, was lying at the bottom of the stream, and when it felt the water disturbed above by the man swimming, suddenly rushed out, and, giving an awful roar, darted after him, with its mouth wide open, as the man swam in the middle of the stream. Then the blessed man observing this, raised his holy hand, while all the rest, brethren as well as strangers, were stupefied with terror, and, invoking the name of God, formed the saving sign of the cross in the air, and commanded the ferocious monster, saying, "Thou shalt go no further, nor touch the man; go back with all speed." Then at the voice of the saint, the monster was terrified, and fled more quickly than if it had been pulled back with ropes, though it had just got so near to Lugne, as he swam, that there was not more than the length of a spear-staff between the man and the beast. Then the brethren seeing that the monster had gone back, and that their comrade Lugne returned to them in the boat safe and sound, were struck with admiration, and gave glory to God in the blessed man. And even the barbarous heathens, who were present, were forced by the greatness of this miracle, which they themselves had seen, to magnify the God of the Christians.

Chapter 29
How the Saint Blessed the Soil of This Island That No Poison of Serpents Should Henceforth Hurt Anyone

On a certain day in that same summer in which he passed to the Lord,[8] the saint went in a chariot to visit some of the brethren, who were engaged in some heavy work in the western part of Iona Island. After speaking to them some words of comfort and encouragement, the saint stood upon the higher ground, and uttered the following prophecy: "My dear children, I know that from this day you shall never see my face again anywhere in this field." Seeing the brethren filled with sorrow upon hearing these words, the saint tried to comfort them as best he could; and, raising both his holy hands, he blessed the whole of this our island, saying: "From this very moment poisonous reptiles shall in no way be able to hurt men or cattle in this island, so long as the inhabitants shall continue to observe the commandments of Christ."

Chapter 30
Of the Knife Which the Saint Blessed

At another time, a certain brother named Molua, grandson of Brian, came to the saint whilst he was writing, and said to him, "This knife which I hold in my hand I beseech thee to bless." The saint, without turning his face from the book out of which he was writing, extended his holy hand a little, with the pen in it, and blessed the knife by signing it. But when the foresaid brother had departed with the knife thus blessed, the saint asked, "What sort of a knife have I blessed for that brother?" Diormit, the saint's faithful attendant, replied, "You have blessed a knife for killing bulls or oxen." The saint then, on the contrary, said, "I trust in my Lord that the knife I have blessed will never wound men or cattle." This word of the holy man received the strongest confirmation the same hour; for the same brother went beyond the enclosure of the monastery and attempted to kill an ox, but, although he made three strong efforts with all his strength, yet he could not even cut the skin. When this came to the knowledge of the monks, they skillfully melted down the iron of the knife and applied a thin coating of it to all the iron tools used in the monastery. And such was the abiding virtue of the saint's blessing, that these tools could never afterwards inflict a wound on flesh.

Chapter 31
Of the Cure of Diormit When Sick

At another time, Diormit, the saint's faithful attendant, was sick even unto death, and the saint went to see him in his extremity. Having invoked the name of Christ, he stood at the bed of the sick man and prayed for him, saying, "O my Lord, be propitious to me, I beseech thee, and take not away the soul of my faithful attendant from its dwelling in the flesh whilst I live." Having said this, he remained silent for a short time, and then again he spoke these words, with his sacred mouth, "My son shall not only not die at present, but will even live for many years after my death." This prayer of the saint was heard, for, on the instant that the saint's prayer was made, Diormit was restored to perfect health, and lived also for many years after St. Columba had passed to the Lord.

Chapter 32
Of the Cure of Finten, the Son of Aid

At another time also, as the saint was making a journey beyond the Dorsal Ridge of Britain (Drumalban), a certain youth named Finten, one of his companions, was seized with a sudden illness and reduced to the last extremity. His comrades were much afflicted on his account, and besought the saint to pray for him. Yielding at once to their entreaties, Columba raised his holy hands to heaven in earnest prayer, and blessing the sick person, said, "This youth for whom you plead shall enjoy a long life; he will survive all who are here present, and die in a good old age." This prophecy of the blessed man was fulfilled in every particular; for this same youth, after founding the monastery of Kailli-au-inde, closed this present life at a good old age.

Chapter 33
Of the Boy Whom the Holy Man Raised From the Dead

At the time when St. Columba was tarrying for some days in the province of the Picts, a certain peasant who, with his whole family, had listened to and learned through an interpreter the word of life preached by the holy man, believed and was baptized the husband, together with his wife, children, and domestics.

A very few days after his conversion, one of the sons of this householder was attacked with a dangerous illness and brought to the very borders of life and death. When the Druids saw him in a dying state they began with great bitterness to upbraid his parents, and to extol their own gods as more powerful than the God of the Christians, and thus to despise God as though He were weaker than their gods. When all this was told to the blessed man, he burned with zeal for God, and proceeded with some of his companions to the house of the friendly peasant, where he found the afflicted parents celebrating the obsequies of their child, who was newly dead. The saint, on seeing their bitter grief, strove to console them with words of comfort, and exhorted them not to doubt in any way the omnipotence of God. He then inquired, saying, "In what chamber is the dead body of your son lying?" And being conducted by the bereaved father under the sad roof, he left the whole crowd of persons who accompanied him outside, and immediately entered by himself into the house of mourning, where, falling on his knees, he prayed to Christ our Lord, having his face bedewed with copious tears. Then rising from his kneeling posture, he turned his eyes towards the deceased and said, "In the name of the Lord Jesus Christ, arise, and stand upon thy feet." At the sound of this glorious word from the saint, the soul returned to the body, and the person that was dead opened his eyes and revived. The apostolic man then taking him by the hand raised him up, and placing him in a standing position, led him forth with him from the house, and restored him to his parents. Upon this the cries of the applauding multitude broke forth, sorrow was turned into joy, and the God of the Christians glorified.

We must thus believe that our saint had the gift of miracles like the prophets Elijah and Elisha, and like the apostles Peter, Paul, and John, he had the honor bestowed on him of raising the dead to life, and now in heaven, placed amid the prophets and apostles, this prophetic and apostolic man enjoys a glorious and eternal throne in the heavenly fatherland with Christ, who reigns with the Father in the unity of the Holy Ghost forever.

Chapter 34
Of the Illness of the Druid Broichan

About the same time the venerable man, from motives of humanity, besought Broichan the Druid to liberate a certain Scotic female slave, and when he very cruelly and obstinately refused to part with her, the saint then spoke to him to the following effect: "Know, O Broichan, and be assured that if thou refuse to set this captive free, as I desire thee, that thou shalt die suddenly before I take my departure again from this province." Having said this in presence of Brude, the king, he departed from the royal palace and proceeded to the river Nesa (the Ness); from this stream he took a white pebble, and showing it to his companions said to them: "Behold this white pebble by which God will affect the cure of many diseases among this heathen nation."

Having thus spoken, he instantly added, "Broichan is chastised grievously at this moment, for an angel being sent from heaven, and striking him severely, hath broken into many pieces the glass cup in his hand from which he was drinking, and hath left him gasping deeply for breath, and half dead. Let us await here a short time, for two of the king's messengers, who have been sent after us in haste, to request us to return quickly and help the dying Broichan, who, now that he is thus terribly punished, will consent to set the girl free."

Whilst the saint was yet speaking, behold, there arrived, as he had predicted, two horsemen who were sent by the king, and who related all that had occurred to Broichan in the royal fortress, according to the prediction of the saint, both the breaking of the drinking goblet, the punishment of the Druid, and his willingness to set his captive at liberty; they then added: "The king and his friends have sent us to thee to request that thou wouldst cure his foster-father Broichan, who is laying in a dying state.

Having heard these words of the messengers, St. Columba sent two of his companions to the king with the pebble which he had blessed, and said to them: "If Broichan shall first promise to set the maiden free, then at once immerse this little stone in water, and let him drink from it and he shall be instantly cured; but if he break his vow and refuse to liberate her, he shall die that instant."

The two persons, in obedience to the saint's instructions, proceeded to the palace, and announced to the king the words of the venerable man. When they were made known to the king and his tutor Broichan, they were so dismayed that they immediately liberated the captive and delivered her to the saint's messengers. The pebble was then immersed in water, and in a wonderful manner, contrary to the laws of nature, the stone floated on the water like a nut or an apple, nor, as it had been blessed by the holy man, could it be submerged. Broichan drank from the stone as it floated on the water, and instantly returning from the verge of death recovered his perfect health and soundness of body.

This remarkable pebble, which was afterwards preserved among the treasures of the king, through the mercy of God affected the cure of sundry diseases among the people, while it in the same manner floated when dipped in water. And what is very wonderful, when this same stone was sought for by those sick persons whose term of life had arrived, it could not be found. Thus, on the very day on which King Brude died, though it was sought for, yet it could not be found in the place where it had been previously laid.

Chapter 35
Of the Manner in Which Saint Columba Overcame Broichan the Druid and Sailed Against the Wind

On a certain day after the events recorded in the foregoing chapters, Broichan, whilst conversing with the saint, said to him: "Tell me, Columba, when do you propose to set sail?" The saint replied, "I intend to begin my voyage after three days, if God permits me, and preserves my life." Broichan said, "On the contrary, thou shalt not be able, for I can make the winds unfavorable to thy voyage, and cause a great darkness to envelop you in its shade." Upon this the saint observed: "The almighty power of God rules all things, and in His name and under His guiding providence all our movements are directed." What more need I say? That same day, the saint, accompanied by a large number of followers, went to the long lake of the river Nesa (Loch Ness), as he had determined. Then the Druids began to exult, seeing that it had become very dark, and that the wind was very violent and contrary. Nor should we wonder, that God sometimes allows them, with the aid of evil spirits, to raise tempests and agitate the sea. For thus legions of demons once met in the midst of the sea the holy bishop Germanus, whilst on his voyage through the Gallican channel to Britain, whither he was going from zeal for the salvation of souls, and exposed him to great dangers, by raising a violent storm and causing great darkness whilst it was yet day. But all these things were dissipated by the prayers of St. Germanus more rapidly than his words were uttered, and the darkness passed away.[9]

Our Columba, therefore, seeing that the sea was violently agitated, and that the wind was most unfavorable for his voyage, called on Christ the Lord and embarked in his small boat; and whilst the sailors hesitated, he the more confidently ordered them to raise the sails against the wind. No sooner was this order executed, while the whole crowd was looking on, than the vessel ran against the wind with extraordinary speed. And after a short time, the wind, which hitherto had been against them, veered round to help them on their voyage, to the intense astonishment of all. And thus throughout the remainder of that day the light breeze continued most favorable, and the skiff of blessed man was carried safely to the wished-for haven.

Let the reader therefore consider how great and eminent this venerable man must have been, upon whom God Almighty, for the purpose of manifesting His illustrious name before a heathen people, bestowed the gift of working such miracles as those we have recorded.

Chapter 36
*Of the Miraculous Opening of the Door of the
Royal Fortress of King Brude*

At another time, when the saint made his first journey to King Brude, it happened that the king, elated by the pride of royalty, acted haughtily, and would not open his gates on the first arrival of the blessed man. When the man of God observed this, he approached the folding doors with his companions, and having first formed upon them the sign of the cross of our Lord, he then knocked at and laid his hand upon the gate, which instantly flew open of its own accord, the bolts having been driven back with great force. The saint and his companions then passed through the gate thus speedily opened. And when the king learned what had occurred, he and his councilors were filled with alarm, and immediately setting out from the palace, he advanced to meet with due respect the blessed man, whom he addressed in the most conciliating and respectful language. And ever after from that day, so long as he lived, the king held this holy and reverend man in very great honor, as was due.

Chapter 37
Of a Similar Unclosing of the Church of the Field of the Two Streams (Tirdaglas, in Tipperary)

Upon another occasion, when the saint was staying a few days in Scotia (Ireland), he went, on invitation, to visit the brethren in the monastery of the Field of the Two Streams (Tirdaglas). But it happened, by some accident, that when he arrived at the church the keys of the oratory could not be found. When the saint observed the brethren lamenting to one another about the keys being astray, and the door locked, he went himself to the door and said, "The Lord is able, without a key, to open his own house for his servants." At these words, the bolts of the lock were driven back with great force, and the door opened of itself. The saint entered the church before all with universal admiration; and he was afterwards most hospitably entertained by the brethren, and treated by all with the greatest respect and veneration.

Chapter 38
Concerning a Certain Peasant Who Was a Beggar, for Whom the Saint Made and Blessed a Stake for Killing Wild Beasts

At another time there came to St. Columba a very poor peasant, who lived in the district which borders the shores of Lochaber. The blessed man, taking pity on the wretched man, who had not wherewithal to support his wife and family, gave him all the alms he could afford, and then said to him, "Poor man, take a branch from the neighboring wood, and bring it to me quickly." The wretched man brought the branch as he was directed, and the saint, taking it in his own hand, sharpened it to a point like a stake, and, blessing it, gave it back to the destitute man, saying, "Preserve this stake with great care, and it, I believe, will never hurt men or cattle, but only wild beasts and fishes; and as long as you preserve this stake thou shalt never be without abundance of venison in thy house."

The wretched beggar upon hearing this was greatly delighted, and returning home, fixed the stake in a remote place which was frequented by the wild beasts of the forest; and when that next night was past, he went at early morning dawn to see the stake, and found a stag of great size that had fallen upon it and been transfixed by it.

Why should I mention more instances? Not a day could pass, so the tradition goes, in which he did not find a stag or hind or some other wild beast fixed upon the stake; and his whole house being thus filled with the flesh of the wild beasts, he sold to his neighbors all that remained after his own family was supplied.

But, as in the case of Adam, the envy of the devil also found out this miserable man also through his wife, who, not as a prudent matron, but rather like one infatuated, thus spoke to her husband: "Remove the stake out of the earth, for if men, or cattle, perish on it, then you and I and our children shall be put to death, or led into captivity." To these words her husband replied, "It will not be so, for when the holy man blessed the stake he said it would never injure men or cattle." Still the miserable man, after saying this, yielded to his wife, and taking the stake out of the earth, like a man deprived of his reason, brought it into the house and placed it against the wall. Soon after his house-dog fell upon it and was killed, and on its death his wife said to him, "One of thy children will fall upon it and be killed." At these words of his wife he removed the stake out of the house, and having carried it to a forest, placed it in the thickest brushwood, where, as he thought, no animal could be hurt by it; but upon his return the following day he found a roe had fallen upon it and perished. He then took it away and concealed it by thrusting it under the water in the edge of the river, which may be called in Latin Nigra Dea. On returning the next day he found transfixed, and still held by it, a salmon of extraordinary size, which he was scarcely able by himself to take from the river and carry home. At the same time, he took the stake again back with him from the water, and placed it outside on the top of his house, where a crow having soon after lighted, was instantly killed by the force of the fall. Upon this the miserable man, yielding again to the advice of his foolish wife, took down the stake from the house-top, and taking an axe cut it in many pieces, and threw them into the fire. Having thus deprived himself of this effectual means of alleviating his distress, he was again, as he deserved to be, reduced to beggary. This freedom from want was owing to the stake, so frequently mentioned above, which the blessed man had blest and given him, and which, so long as it was kept, could suffice for snares and nets, and every kind of fishing and hunting; but when the stake was lost, the wretched peasant, though he had been enriched for the time, could only, when too late, lament over it with his whole family all the rest of his life.

Chapter 39
Concerning a Certain Leather Vessel

On another occasion, when the blessed man's messenger, who was named Lugaid, and surnamed Laitir, was at his command making preparations for a voyage to Scotia (Ireland), he searched for and found amongst the sea- going articles that belonged to the saint's ship a leather vessel for holding milk. This vessel he immersed in the sea in order to moisten it, and put upon it stones of considerable size. He then went to the saint, and told him what he had done with the leather bottle.

The saint smiled and said, "I do not think that this vessel, which you say you have sunk under the waves, will accompany thee to Hibernia on the present occasion." "Why," rejoined Lugaid, "can I not take it with me in the ship?" The saint replied, "You shall learn the reason tomorrow, as the event will prove."

On the following morning, therefore, Lugaid went to take the vessel out of the sea, but the ebb of the tide had carried it away during the night. When he could not find it, he returned in grief to the saint, and on his bended knees on the ground confessed his negligence. St. Columba consoled him, saying, "My brother, grieve not for perishable things. The vessel which the ebbing tide has carried away the returning tide will, after your departure, bring back to the spot where you did place it." At the ninth hour of the same day, soon after the departure of Lugaid from Iona, the saint addressed those who stood near him, and said, "Let one of you now go to the sea, for the leather vessel for which Lugaid was lamenting, when it was carried away by the ebbing tide, hath been brought back by the returning tide, and is to be found at the place from which it was taken." Upon hearing these words spoken by the saint, a certain active youth ran to the sea-shore, where he found the vessel, as the saint had predicted. He immediately took it out of the water, and with great joy hastened back at full speed to the holy man, into whose hands he delivered it, amid the great admiration of all the beholders.

In the two miracles which we have just recorded, and which regard such common and trifling things as a wooden stake and a leather vessel, there may, nevertheless, be observed, as we noticed before, the gift of prophecy united with the power of working miracles.

Let us now proceed with our narrative regarding other things.

Chapter 40
The Saint's Prophecy Regarding Libran

At another time, while the saint was living in Iona, a certain man of humble birth, who had lately assumed the clerical habit, sailed over from Scotia (Ireland), and came to the blessed man's monastery on the island. The saint found him one day sitting alone in the lodging provided for strangers, and inquired first about his country, family, and the object of his journey. He replied that he was born in the region of Connaught, and that he had undertaken that long and weary journey to atone for his sins by the pilgrimage.

In order to test the depth of his repentance, the saint then laid down minutely before his eyes the hardship and labor attending the monastic exercises. "I am prepared," he replied at once to the saint, "to do everything whatever thou dost bid me, however hard and however humiliating." Why add more? That same hour he confessed all his sins, and promised, kneeling on the ground, to fulfil the laws of penance. The saint said to him, "Arise and take a seat." Then he thus addressed him as he sat, "Thou must do penance for seven years in the land of Tiree; thou and I, with God's blessing, shall survive that period of seven years." Being comforted by the saint's words, he first gave thanks to God, and turning afterwards to the saint, asked, "What am I to do with regard to an oath which I have violated? For while living in my own country I murdered a certain man, and afterwards, as guilty of murdering him, I was confined in prison. But a certain very wealthy blood-relation came to my aid, and promptly loosing me from my prison-chains, rescued me from the death to which I was condemned. When I was released, I bound myself by oath to serve that friend all the days of my life; but I had remained only a short time in his service, when I felt ashamed of serving man, and very much preferred to devote myself to God. I therefore left that earthly master, broke the oath, and departing, reached thee safely, God prospering my journey thus far."

The saint, on seeing him very much grieved over such things, and first prophesying with respect to him, thus made answer, saying, "At the end of seven years, as I said to thee, thou shalt come to me here during the forty days of Lent, and thou shalt approach the altar and partake of the Eucharist at the great Paschal festival." Why hang longer over words? The penitent stranger in every respect obeyed the saint's commands; and being sent at that time to the monastery of the Plain of Lunge (Magh Lunge, in Tiree), and having fully completed his seven years' penance there, returned to him during Lent, according to the previous command and prophecy. After celebrating the Paschal solemnity, and coming at that time to the altar as directed, he came again to the saint to consult him on the above-mentioned oath. Then the saint gave this prophetic answer to his inquiry, "That earthly master of thine of whom thou hast formerly spoken is still living; so are thy father, thy mother, and thy brethren. Thou must now, therefore, prepare thyself for the voyage." And while speaking, he drew forth a sword ornamented with carved ivory, and said, "Take this gift to carry with thee, and offer it to thy master as the price of thy ransom; but when you do, he will on no account accept it, for he has a virtuous, kindly-disposed wife, and by the influence of her wholesome counsel he shall that very day, without recompense or ransom, set thee free, unbinding the girdle round thy captive loins. But though thus relieved from this anxiety, you shalt not escape a source of disquietude arising on another hand, for thy brethren will come round and press thee to make good the support due to thy father for so long a time which thou hast neglected. Comply at once with their wish, and take in hand dutifully to cherish your aged father. Though the duty may, indeed, seem weighty, you must not be grieved thereat, because you shalt soon be relieved of it; for from the day on which you shalt take charge of thy father, the end of that same week shall see his death and burial. But after thy father's burial thy brethren will a second time come and sharply demand of thee that thou pay the expenses due for thy mother. However, thy younger brother will assuredly set thee free from this necessity by engaging to perform in thy stead every duty or obligation which you owe to thy mother."

Having heard these words, the above-mentioned brother, whose name was Libran, received the gift, and set out enriched with the saint's blessing. When he reached his native country, he found everything exactly as prophesied by the saint. For when he showed and made offer of the price of his freedom to his master, his wife opposed his wish to accept it, saying, "What need have we to accept this ransom sent by St. Columba? We are not even worthy of such a favor. Release this dutiful servant without payment. The prayers of the holy man will profit us more than this price which is offered us." The husband, therefore, listening to his wife's wholesome counsel, set the slave free at once without ransom. He was afterwards, according to the saint's prophecy, compelled by his brethren to undertake the providing for his father, and he buried him at his death on the seventh day. After his burial they required him to discharge the same duty to his mother; but a younger brother, as the saint foretold, engaged to supply his place, and thus released him from the obligation. "We ought not on any account," said he to his brethren," detain this our brother at home, who, for the salvation of his soul, has spent seven years in penitential exercises with St. Columba in Britain."

After being thus released from the matters which gave him annoyance, he bade farewell to his mother and brothers, and returned a free man to a place called in the Scotic tongue Daire Calgaich (Derry). There he found a ship under sail just leaving the harbor, and he called to the sailors to take him on board and convey him to Britain. But they, not being the monks of

St. Columba, refused to receive him. He then prayed to the venerable man, who, though far distant, indeed, in body, yet was present in spirit, as the event soon proved, saying, "Is it thy will, holy Columba, that these sailors, who do not receive me, thy companion, proceed upon their voyage with full sails and favorable winds?"

At this saying the wind, which till then was favorable for them, veered round on the instant to the opposite point. While this was taking place, the sailors saw again the same man running in a line with them along the bank of the river, and, hastily taking counsel together, they cried out to him from the ship, saying, "Perhaps the wind hath suddenly turned against us, for this reason, that we refused to give thee a passage; but if even now we were to invite thee to be with us on board, could you change these contrary winds to be in our favor?" When the pilgrim heard this, he said to them, "St. Columba, to whom I am going, and whom I have served for the last seven years, is able by prayer, if you take me on board, to obtain a favorable wind for you from his Lord." They then on hearing this, approached the land with their ship, and asked him to join them in it. As soon as he came on board, he said, "In the name of the Almighty God, whom St. Columba blamelessly serves, spread your sails on the extended yards." And when they had done so, the gale of contrary winds immediately became favorable, and the vessel made a prosperous voyage under full sail to Britain.

After reaching the shores of Britain, Libran left the ship, blessed the sailors, and went directly to St. Columba, who was staying on Iona. The blessed man welcomed him with joy, and, without receiving the information from any one, told him fully of everything that happened on his way: of his master and the wife's kindly suggestion and of his being set free by her advice; of his brethren also, and the death and burial of his father within the week; of his mother, and the timely assistance of the younger brother; of what occurred as he was returning, the adverse and favorable winds; of the words of the sailors when first they refused to take him in; of the promise of fair wind, and of the favorable change when they took him on board their vessel. Why need I add more? Every particular the saint foretold he now described after it was exactly fulfilled.

After these words, the traveler gave back to the saint the price of his ransom which he had received from him; and at the same time the saint addressed him in these words: "Inasmuch as thou art free, thou shalt be called Libran."[10] Libran took at the same period the monastic vows with much fervor.

And when he was being sent back again by the holy man to the monastery where he had formerly served the Lord during the seven years of penance, he received in farewell the following prophetic announcement regarding himself: "Thou shalt live yet a long time, and end this present life in a good old age; yet thou shalt not arise from the dead in Britain, but in Scotia (Ireland)." Hearing these words, he knelt down and wept bitterly. When the saint saw his great grief he tried to comfort him, saying, "Arise, and be not sad. Thou shalt die in one of my monasteries, and thy lot shall be among my chosen monks in the kingdom; and with them thou shalt awake from the sleep of death unto the resurrection of life." When he heard this unusual consolation from the saint he rejoiced exceedingly, and, being enriched by the saint's blessing, went away in peace.

This truthful prophecy of the saint regarding the same man was afterwards fulfilled; for when he had faithfully served the Lord for many revolving years of holy obedience in the monastery of the Plain of Lunge (Magh Lunge, in Tiree), after the departure of St. Columba from the world, he was sent, in extreme old age, on a mission to Ireland regarding the interests of the monastery, and proceeded as soon as he landed through the Plain of Breg (Maghbreg, in Meath), till he reached the monastery of the

Oakwood Plain (Derry). Being there received as a stranger in the guest-chamber, and suffering from a certain disease, he passed to the Lord in peace on the seventh day of his illness, and was buried with the chosen monks of St. Columba, according to his prophecy, to await the resurrection unto eternal life.

Let it suffice that we have written these truthful prophecies of St. Columba regarding Libran of the Rush-ground. He was called "of the Rush-ground" from his having been engaged many years in the labor of collecting rushes.

Chapter 41
Concerning a Certain Little Woman who was Enduring the Great and Extremely Dangerous Pains of Childbirth

On a certain day during the saint's stay on Iona island, the saint arose from reading, and said with a smile, "I must now hasten to the oratory to pray to the Lord on behalf of a poor woman in Hibernia, who at this moment is suffering the pangs of a most difficult childbirth, and is calling upon the name of Columba. She trusts that God will grant her relief from her sufferings through my prayers, because she is a relation of mine, being lineally descended from the house of my mother's parentage."

Having said this, the saint, being touched with pity for the poor woman, hastened to the church, and, on his bended knees, earnestly prayed for her to Christ, who was Himself by birth a partaker of humanity. Returning from the church after his prayer, he said to the brethren who met him, "The Lord Jesus, born of a woman, has given seasonable help to this poor woman, and has mercifully relieved her from her distress. She has been safely delivered of a child, nor shall she die upon this occasion." That same hour, as the saint had predicted, the poor woman, by invoking his name, was safely delivered, and restored to perfect health, as we afterwards learned from travelers who came to us from that part of Scotia (Ireland) where the woman resided.

Chapter 42
Of one Lugne, Who Being Deformed, His Wife Hated

Another time, when the saint was living on the Rechrean island, a certain man of humble birth came to him and complained of his wife, who, as he said, so hated him, that she would on no account allow him to come near her for marriage rights. The saint on hearing this, sent for the wife, and, so far as he could, began to reprove her on that account, saying: "Why, O woman, do you endeavor to withdraw thy flesh from thyself, while the Lord says, 'They shall be two in one flesh'? Wherefore the flesh of thy husband is thy flesh." She answered and said, "Whatever you shall require of me I am ready to do, however hard it may be, with this single exception: that you dost not urge me in any way to sleep in one bed with Lugne. I do not refuse to perform every duty at home, or, if you command me, even to pass over the seas, or to live in some monastery for women." The saint then said, "What you propose cannot be lawfully done, for you are bound by the law of the husband as long as your husband lives, for it would be impious to separate those whom God has lawfully joined together." Immediately after these words he added: "This day let us three, namely, the husband and his wife and myself, join in prayer to the Lord and in fasting." But the woman replied: "I know it is not impossible for you to obtain from God, when you ask them, those things that seem to us either difficult, or even impossible." It is unnecessary to say more. The husband and wife agreed to fast with the saint that day, and the following night the saint spent sleepless in prayer for them. Next day he thus addressed the wife in presence of her husband, and said to her: "O woman, art thou still ready to-day, as thou saidst yesterday, to go away to a convent of women?" "I know now," she answered, "that thy prayer to God for me has been heard; for that man whom I hated yesterday, I love today; for my heart hath been changed last night in some unknown way—from hatred to love." Why need we linger over it? From that day to the hour of death, the soul of the wife was firmly cemented in affection to her husband, so that she no longer refused those mutual matrimonial rights which she was formerly unwilling to allow.

Chapter 43
Prophecy of Columba Regarding the Voyage of Cormac

At another time a soldier of Christ, named Cormac, about whom we have related a few brief particulars in the first part of this book, made even a second attempt to discover a desert in the ocean. After he had gone far from the land over the boundless ocean at full sail, St. Columba, who was then staying beyond the Dorsal Ridge of Britain (Drumalban), recommended him in the following terms to King Brude, in the presence of the ruler of the Orcades (Orkneys): "Some of our brethren have lately set sail, and are anxious to discover a desert in the pathless sea; should they happen, after many wanderings, to come to the Orcadian islands, do thou carefully instruct this chief, whose hostages are in your hand, that no evil befall them within his dominions." The saint took care to give this direction, because he knew that after a few months Cormac would arrive at the Orcades. So it afterwards came to pass, and to this advice of the holy man Cormac owed his escape from impending death.

After the lapse of a few months, whilst the saint was remaining in Iona, Cormac's name was mentioned one day unexpectedly in his presence by some persons in conversation, who were observing that it was not yet known whether the voyage of Cormac had been successful or otherwise. Upon hearing this, the saint joined the conversation and said: "You shall see Cormac, about whom you are now speaking, arrive here today."

And after about an hour, wonderful to relate, lo! Cormac unexpectedly arrived, and proceeded to the oratory whilst all expressed their admiration and gave thanks to God.

Having mentioned thus briefly the prediction of the blessed man regarding Cormac's second voyage, we have now to relate another equally remarkable instance of the holy man's prophetic knowledge regarding his third voyage.

When Cormac was laboriously engaged in his third voyage over the ocean, he was exposed to the most imminent danger of death. For, when for fourteen days in summer, and as many nights, his vessel sailed with full sails before a south wind, in a straight course from land, into the northern regions, his voyage seemed to be extended beyond the limits of human wanderings, and return to be impossible.

Accordingly, after the tenth hour of the fourteenth day, certain dangers of a most formidable and almost insurmountable kind presented themselves. A multitude of loathsome and annoying insects, such as had never been seen before, covered the sea in swarms, and struck the keel and sides, the prow, and stern of the vessel, so very violently, that it seemed as if they would wholly penetrate the leathern covering of the ship. According to the accounts afterwards-given by those who were there, they were about the size of frogs; they could swim, but were not able to fly; their sting was extremely painful, and they crowded upon the handles of the oars.

When Cormac and his fellow-voyagers had seen these and other monsters, which it is not now our province to describe, they were filled with fear and alarm, and, shedding copious tears, they prayed to God, who is a kind and ready helper of those who are in trouble. At that same hour our holy Columba, although far away in body, was present in spirit with Cormac in the ship. Accordingly he gave the signal, and calling the brethren to the oratory, he entered the church, and addressing those who were present, he uttered the following prophecy in his usual manner: "Brethren, pray with all your usual fervor for Cormac, who by sailing too far has passed the bounds of human enterprise, and is exposed at this moment to dreadful alarm and fright, in the presence of monsters which were never before seen, and are almost indescribable. We ought, therefore, to sympathize with our brethren and associates who are in such imminent danger, and to pray to the Lord with them; behold at this moment Cormac and his sailors are shedding copious tears. And praying with intense fervency to Christ; let us assist them by our prayers, that God may take compassion upon us, and cause the wind, which for the past fourteen days has blown from the south, to blow from the north, and this north wind will, of course, deliver Cormac's vessel out of all danger."

Having said this he knelt before the altar, and in a plaintive voice poured forth his prayers to the almighty power of God, who governs the winds and all things. After having prayed he arose quickly, and wiping away his tears, joyfully gave thanks to God, saying, "Now, brethren, let us congratulate our dear friends for whom we have been praying, for God will now change the south into a north wind, which will free our associates from their perils, and bring them to us here again." As he spoke the south wind ceased, and a north wind blew for many days after, so that Cormac's ship was enabled to gain the land. And Cormac hastened to visit Columba, and in God's bounty they looked on each other again face to face, to the extreme joy and wonder of all. Let the reader, then, carefully consider how great and of what a character the blessed man must have been, who possessed such prophetic knowledge, and who, by invoking the name of Christ, could rule the winds and the waves.

Chapter 44
How the Venerable Man Made a Journey in a Chariot Which was not Secured With the Proper Lynch-pins

At another time, while the saint was spending a few days in Scotia (Ireland), some ecclesiastical object required his presence, and accordingly he ascended a yoked car which he had previously blessed; but from some unaccountable neglect the requisite lynch-pins were not inserted in the holes at the extremities of the axles. The person who on this occasion performed the duty of driver in the carriage with St. Columba was Columban, a holy man, the son of Echud, and founder of that monastery which is called in the Scotic language Snam luthir (now Slanore, in Granard, county of Longford).[11] The distance they rode that day was very long, and the jolting severe, yet the wheels did not come off the axles nor even stir from their proper places, although, as was mentioned before, there were no lynch-pins to secure them. But divine grace alone so favored the venerable man that the car in which he was safely seated proceeded without being upset, or meeting any obstacle to retard its progress.

Thus far we may have written enough regarding the miracles which the divine omnipotence wrought through this remarkable man while he lived; we shall now mention also a few out of many well-authenticated miracles which the Lord was pleased to grant to him after his death.

Chapter 45
Of the Rain Which, After Some Months of Drought, the Lord Bountifully Poured Out Upon the Earth in Honor of the Blessed Man

About fourteen years before the date at which we write, there occurred during the spring a very great and long-continued drought in these marshy regions, insomuch that the threat denounced against sinners in the Book of Leviticus seemed to impend over the people: "I will give to you the heaven above as iron, and the earth as brass. Your labor shall be spent in vain, the ground shall not bring forth her increase, nor the trees their fruit," etc.[12]

We therefore, reading these words, and fearing the impending calamity, took counsel together, and resolved that some of the senior members of the community should walk round a newly ploughed and sowed field, taking with them the white tunic of St. Columba, and some books written in his own hand, that they should raise in the air, and shake three times the tunic which the saint wore at the hour of his death; and that they then should open the books and read them on the little hill of the angels (now called Sithean Mor), where the citizens of the heavenly country were occasionally seen to descend at the bidding of the blessed man. When these directions had been executed in the manner prescribed, then, strange to relate, the sky, which during the preceding months of March and April had been cloudless, was suddenly covered with dense vapors that arose from the sea with extraordinary rapidity; copious rain fell day and night, and the parched earth being sufficiently moistened, produced its fruits in good season, and yielded the same year a most abundant harvest. And thus the invocation of the very name of the blessed man, by the exhibition of his tunic and books, obtained seasonable relief at the same time for many places and much people.

Chapter 46
Of the Unfavorable Winds Which Were Changed Into Propitious Breezes

Our belief in the miracles which we have recorded, but which we did not ourselves see, is confirmed beyond doubt by the miracles of which we were eye-witnesses; for on three different occasions we saw unfavorable gales of wind changed unto propitious breezes.

On the first occasion we had to draw over land long boats of hewn pine and oak, and to bring home in the same way a large quantity of materials for building ships. In order to obtain from the Lord a favorable wind for our voyage, we took counsel and put the books and garments of the blessed man upon the altar, and at the same time fasted, chanted psalms, and invoked his name.

And this was granted to the holy man by God's favor, for on the day that our sailors had made all their preparations, and were ready to convey the wood for the purposes above mentioned in curachs[13] and skiffs, the wind, which for several days before had been contrary, suddenly changed into favorable breezes. They blew steadily the entire day, by God's blessing, and enabled the whole fleet of boats to make their long and dangerous passage to Iona, with safety and expedition.

On the second occasion, which was a few years after the one just mentioned, our monastery was requiring repairs, and some oak-trees were to be taken from near the mouth of the river Sale (the Seil, in Lorn), in twelve vessels which we brought for the purpose. Our sailors then rowed out to sea with their oars, the day being calm and the sea tranquil, when suddenly a westerly wind, which is also called Zephyr, sprang up, and we betook ourselves to the nearest island, which is called in Scotic Airthrago (probably Kerrera), to seek for shelter in a harbor in it.

But in the meantime we began to complain of this unfavorable change in the wind, and in some measure even to blame our Columba, saying, "Does our unfortunate detention in this place please thee, O saint? Hitherto we had hoped that we might receive from you some aid and comfort in our labors through the divine favor, seeing we thought that you were honored and powerful in the sight of God."

No sooner had we thus spoken, than, wonderful to relate, the unfavorable west wind ceased, and immediately, in the course as it were of one minute, behold a most favorable south-eastern breeze sprang up. The sailors were then directed to raise the sail yards in the form of a cross, and spread the sails upon them; thus putting to sea with a steady and favorable breeze, we were enabled, without the slightest fatigue, to reach our island that same day, rejoicing in our cargo of wood, and in the company of all who were engaged in assisting us in the ships. Thus the chiding with the holy man, slight though it was, in that complaint assisted us not a little; and in what and how great esteem the saint is held by the Lord is evident from His hearing him so quickly and changing the winds.

Then the third instance was in the summer, after the celebration of a synod in Hibernia, when we were detained by contrary winds for a few days among the people of the tribe of Loern (Lorn), and had reached the Sainean island (Shuna). There the vigil and the feast of St. Columba found us extremely sad and disconsolate, because we wished to celebrate that joyous day on Iona. Accordingly, as on a former occasion, we began to complain and to say, "Is it agreeable to you, O saint, that we should spend tomorrow, thy festival-day, among strangers, and not celebrate it in your own church? It is easy for you in the morning of such a day to obtain from the Lord that the contrary winds may become favorable, and that we may be able to celebrate the solemn mass of your birth in your own church." On the following morning we arose at daybreak, and seeing that the adverse winds had ceased, we went on board our vessels and put to sea in a profound calm, when, lo! There suddenly sprung up a south wind, which was most favorable for the voyage. The sailors then joyously raised the sails, and on this occasion also without any exertion on our part, so quick and so favorable was our passage, owing to the mercy of God to the blessed man, that we reached the landing-place of Iona after the third hour, according to our previous anxious desire. After washing our hands and feet we entered the church at the sixth hour in company with our brethren, and celebrated at once the holy services of the mass of St. Columba and St. Baithene, whose festivals occurred on that day, at the daybreak of which, as we said above, we started: from the distant Sainean island.

And as to the truth of this story I have now related, there are yet living, not merely one or two witnesses as the law requires, but hundreds and more who can bear testimony.

Chapter 47
Concerning the Plague[14]

What we are about to relate concerning the plague, which in our own time twice visited the greater part of the world, deserves, I think, to be reckoned among not the least of the miracles of St. Columba. For, not to mention the other and greater countries of Europe, including Italy, the Roman States, and the Cisalpine provinces of Gaul, with the States of Spain also, which lie beyond the Pyrenees, these islands of the sea, Scotia (Ireland) and Britain, have twice been ravaged by a dreadful pestilence throughout their whole extent, except among the two tribes, the Picts and Scots of Britain, who are separated from each other by the Dorsal mountains of Britain. And although neither of these nations was free from those grievous crimes which generally provoke the anger of the eternal Judge, yet both have been hitherto patiently borne with and mercifully spared. Now, to what other person can this favor granted them by God be attributed unless to St. Columba, whose monasteries lie within the territories of both these people, and have been regarded by both with the greatest respect up to the present time? But what I am now to say cannot, I think, be heard without a sigh, that there are many very stupid people in both countries who, in their ignorance that they owe their exemption from the plague to the prayers of the saint, ungratefully and wickedly abuse the patience and the goodness of God. But I often return my most grateful thanks to God for having, through the intercession of our holy patron, preserved me and those in our islands from the ravages of the pestilence; and that in Saxonia also, when I went to visit my friend King Aldfrid,[15] where the plague was raging and laying waste many of his villages, yet both in its first attack, immediately after the war of Ecfridus, and in its second, two years subsequently, the Lord mercifully saved me from danger, though I was living and moving about in the very midst of the plague. The Divine mercy was also extended to my companions, not one of whom died of the plague, or was attacked with any other disease.

Here must end the second Book recording the miracles, and it is right for me to draw attention to the fact, that many well-authenticated miracles have been omitted in order not to fatigue the reader.

Here endeth the Second Book.

Book Two Notes

1 Findbarr and Vinnian are both other names for St. Finnian of Movilla, St. Columba's teacher. Why two different names for him are used in the same chapter is uncertain. "Findbarr" means "white-headed" and is a nickname; "Vinnian" is a form of "Vennianus", the Latinized version of Finnian.

2 Lat: "The Great Fortress"

3 Cainnech is the famous St. Canice, also known as St. Kenneth in Scotland (d. 600).

4 This does not appear to be the more famous St. Columbán (Columbanus) of Bobbio, who did not die until 615, eighteen years after the death of St. Columba of Iona.

5 In Book II: 23

6 In Latin, "Right-Handed"

7 This is the most famous episode out of the *Life of St. Columba* concerning the first recorded encounter with the famous Loch Ness monster.

8 St. Columba died on June 9, 597. The similarity between this episode and the famous legend of St. Patrick driving the serpents from Ireland should be noted.

9 St. Germanus of Auxerre, d. 448

10 A pun on the Latin word *liberare*, "to free"

11 Not the famous St. Columbanus of Bobbio, but rather St. Colman mac Echdach.

12 Leviticus 26:19

13 Currachs were a type of Irish boat with a wooden frame, over which animal skins or hides were stretched.

14 The famous Plague of Justinian, which initially struck Europe in 541-542 and continued to reoccur for nearly two centuries.

15 King Aldfrid of Northumbria (r. 685-705), a close friend of St. Adomnán, who was pivotal in getting Adomnan to adopt the Roman monastic usages.

Book Three
Of the Visions of the Angels

Chapter 1
Outline of Book Three

In the first of these three little books we have, under the
guidance of God, shortly and concisely related, as was
observed before, some of the prophetic revelations. In the
second we have recorded the powerful miracles the blessed man
wrought, which, as we have often observed, were generally
accompanied with the gift of prophecy. But in this third book,
which treats of the apparitions of angels, we shall relate those
which either our saint received regarding others, or others saw
regarding him; we shall also describe some which were
manifested to both parties, though in different measure, that is,
to the saint himself, specially and clearly, but to the others
improperly and partially, or, in other words, externally and
tentatively, yet in the same visions either of angels, or of
heavenly light. Whatever discrepancies however in any case
may at first sight seem to occur in those visions, will be
completely removed as we proceed to relate them in their
proper places. But now we must begin at the very birth of the
blessed man, and relate these angelic manifestations.

Chapter 2
Of the Birth of Saint Columba

On a certain night between the conception and birth of the venerable man, an angel of the Lord appeared to his mother in dreams, bringing to her, as he stood by her, a certain robe of extraordinary beauty, in which the most beautiful colors, as it were, of all the flowers seemed to be portrayed. After a short time he asked it back, and took it out of her hands, and having raised it and spread it out, he let it fly through the air. But she being sad at the loss of it, said to that man of venerable aspect, "Why do you take this lovely cloak away from me so soon?" He immediately replied, "Because this mantle is so exceedingly honorable that you cannot not retain it longer with thee." When this was said, the woman saw that the fore-mentioned robe was gradually receding from her in its flight; and that then it expanded until its width exceeded the plains, and in all its measurements was larger than the mountains and forests. Then she heard the following words: "Woman, do not grieve, for to the man to whom you have been joined by the marriage bond, you shall bring forth a son, of so beautiful a character, that he shall be reckoned among his own people as one of the prophets of God, and has been predestined by God to be the leader of innumerable souls to the heavenly country." At these words the woman awoke from her sleep.

Chapter 3
Of the Ray of Light on the Boy's Face As He Lay Asleep

On another night, Cruithnecan, a priest of blameless life, to whose care the blessed youth was confided, upon returning home from the church after mass, found his house illuminated with a bright light, and saw in fact a ball of fire standing over the face of the little boy as he lay asleep. At the sight he at once shook with fear, and fell down with his face to the ground in great amazement, well knowing that it indicated the grace of the Holy Spirit poured out from heaven upon his young charge.

Chapter 4
Of the Apparition of Holy Angels Whom Saint Brenden
Saw With the Blessed Man Through the Plain

For indeed after the lapse of many years, when St. Columba was excommunicated by a certain synod for some pardonable and very trifling reasons, and indeed unjustly, as it afterwards appeared at the end, he came to the' same meeting convened against himself.[1] When St. Brenden,[2] the founder of the monastery which in the Scotic language is called Birra (Birr, in King's County), saw him approaching in the distance, he quickly arose, and with head bowed down reverently kissed him.

When some of the seniors in that assembly, going apart from the rest, were finding fault with him, and saying: "Why did you not decline to rise in presence of an excommunicated person, and to kiss him?" he replied to them in this wise: "If," said he, "you had seen what the Lord has this day thought fit to show to me regarding this his chosen one, whom you dishonor, you would never have excommunicated a person whom God not only does not excommunicate, according to your unjust sentence, but even more and more highly esteems."

"How, we would wish to know," said they in reply, "does God exalt, as you say, one whom we have excommunicated, not without reason?"

"I have seen," said Brenden, "a most brilliant pillar wreathed with fiery tresses preceding this same man of God whom you treat with contempt; I have also seen holy angels accompanying him on his journey through the plain. Therefore I do not dare to slight him whom I see foreordained by God to be the leader of his people to life."

When he said this, they desisted, and so far from daring to hold the saint any longer excommunicated, they even treated him with the greatest respect and reverence. This took place in Teilte (Teltown, in Meath).

Chapter 5
The Journey of the Blessed Columba

On another occasion the holy man went to the venerable Bishop Finnio, who had formerly been his preceptor, the youth to visit the man far advanced in years.[3] When St. Finnio saw him coming to him, he observed also an angel of the Lord accompanying him, as he proceeded, and as it is handed down to us by well-informed persons, he made it known to certain brethren who were standing by, saying to them: "Behold, look now to Columba as he draws near; he has been deemed worthy of having an angelic inhabitant of heaven to be his companion in his wanderings." About that same time the holy man, with his twelve disciples and fellow-soldiers, sailed across to Britain.

Chapter 6
Of the Angel and King Aidan

On another occasion, when this eminent man was staying in the Hinba island (Eilean-na-Naoimh), he saw, on a certain night, in a mental ecstasy, an angel sent to him from heaven, and holding in his hand a book of glass, regarding the appointment of kings.

Having received the book from the hand of the angel, the venerable man, at his command, began to read it; and when he was reluctant to appoint Aidan king, as the book directed, because he had a greater affection for Iogenan his brother, the angel, suddenly stretching forth his hand, struck the saint with a scourge, the livid marks of which remained in his side all the days of his life. And he added these words: "Know for certain," said he, "that I am sent to thee by God with the book of glass, that in accordance with the words thou hast read therein, thou mayest inaugurate Aidan into the kingdom; but if thou refuse to obey this command, I will strike thee again."

When therefore this angel of the Lord had appeared for three successive nights, having the same book of glass in his hand, and had repeated the same commands of the Lord regarding the appointment of the same king, the saint, in obedience to the command of the Lord, sailed across to the Iona, and there ordained, as he had been commanded, Aidan to be king, who had arrived at the same time as the saint. During the words of consecration, the saint declared the future regarding the children, grandchildren and great- grandchildren of Aidan, and laying his hand upon his head, he consecrated and blessed him.[4]

Cummene the Fair, in the book which he wrote on the virtues of St. Columba, states that St. Columba commenced his predictions regarding Aidan and his children and kingdom in the following manner: "Believe me, unhesitatingly, O Aidan," said he, "none of thine enemies shall be able to resist thee, unless thou first act unjustly towards me and my successors. Wherefore direct thou thy children to commend to their children, their grandchildren, and their posterity, not to let the sceptre pass out of their hands through evil counsels. For at whatever time they turn against me or my relatives who are in Hibernia, the scourge which I suffered on thy account from the angel shall bring great disgrace upon them by the hand of God, and the hearts of men shall be turned away from them, and their foes shall be greatly strengthened against them."

Now this prophecy hath been fulfilled in our own times in the battle of Roth[5,] in which Domnall Brecc, the grandson of Aidan, ravaged without the slightest provocation the territory of Domnall, the grandson of Ainmuireg. And from that day to this they have been trodden down by strangers, a fate which pierces the heart with sighs and grief.

Chapter 7
Of the Angels Carrying to Heaven the Soul of the Blessed Brito

At another time while the holy man was tarrying at Iona, one of his monks called Brito, a person given to all good works, being seized with bodily illness, was reduced to the last extremity. When the venerable man went to visit him at the hour of his departure, he stood for a few moments at his bedside, and after giving him his blessing, retired quickly from the house, not wishing to see him die, and the very moment after the holy man left the house the monk closed this present life.

Then the eminent man walking in the little court of his monastery, with his eyes upraised to heaven, was for a long time lost in wonder and admiration. But a certain brother named Aidan, the son of Libir, a truly virtuous and religious man, who was the only one of the brethren present at the time, fell upon his knees and asked the saint to tell him the reason of so great astonishment. The saint said to him in reply: "I have this moment seen the holy angels contending in the air against the hostile powers; and I return thanks to Christ, the Judge, because the victorious angels have carried off to the joys of our heavenly country the soul of this stranger, who is the first person that has died among us in this island. But I beseech you not to reveal this secret to any one during my life."

Chapter 8
Concerning the Bearing to Heaven the Soul of One Named Diormit

At another time a stranger from Hibernia came to the saint and remained with him for some months on Iona. The blessed man one day said to him: "One of the clerics of your province, whose name I do not yet know, is being carried to heaven by the angels at this moment." Then the brother, upon hearing this, began to search within himself regarding the province of the Anterii (Airthir), which is called in Scotic Indairthir (East Oriel, in Ulster), and also about the name of that blessed man, and in due course thus expressed himself, saying: "I know a soldier of Jesus Christ, named Diormit, who built a small monastery in the same district where I dwelt." The saint said to him, "The one of whom you speak is the very person who has been carried into Paradise by the angels of God."

But this fact must be very carefully noted, that our venerable man was most careful to conceal from the knowledge of men many mysterious secrets which were concealed from others, but revealed to him by God, and this he did for two reasons, as he one day hinted to a few of the brethren; first, that he might avoid vainglory, and secondly that he might not by the fame of his revelations being spread abroad, attract, to make inquiries at him, innumerable crowds who were anxious to ask some questions regarding themselves.

Chapter 9
Of the Brave Fight of the Angels Against the Demons

On another day while the holy man was living in Iona, he went to seek in the woods for a place more remote from men and fitting for prayer. And there when he began to pray, he suddenly beheld, as he afterwards told a few of the brethren, a very black host of demons fighting against him with iron darts. These wicked demons wished, as the Holy Spirit revealed to the saint, to attack his monastery and kill with the same spears many of the brethren. But he, single-handed, against innumerable foes of such a nature, fought with the utmost bravery, having received the armor of the apostle Paul. And thus the contest was maintained on both sides during the greater part of the day, nor could the demons, countless though they were, vanquish him, nor was he able, by himself, to drive them from his island, until the angels of God, as the saint afterwards told certain persons, and they few in number, came to his aid, when the demons in terror gave way.

On the same day, when the saint was returning to his monastery, after he had driven the devils from his island, he spoke these words concerning the same hostile legions, saying, "Those deadly foes, who this day, through the mercy of God and the assistance of his angels, have been put to flight from this small track of land, have fled to the Ethican land (Tiree), and there as savage invaders they will attack the monasteries of the brethren, and cause pestilential diseases, of which many will be grievously ill and die." All this came to pass in those days, as the blessed man had foreseen.

And two days after he thus spoke from the revelation of the Holy Ghost, "Baithen has managed wisely, with God's help, that the congregation of the church over which he has been appointed by God to preside, in the plain of Lunge (Magh Lunge, in Tiree), should be defended by fasts and prayers against the attacks of the demons, and but one person shall die on this occasion." The whole took place as was foretold; for whilst many in the other monasteries of the same island fell victims to that disease, none except the one of whom the saint spoke died in the congregation which was under the charge of Baithen.

Chapter 10
Of the Apparition of Angels Carrying to Heaven the Soul of the Blacksmith Columb Coilrigin

A certain blacksmith, greatly devoted to works of charity, and full of other good works, dwelt in the midland districts of Scotia (Ireland). When the fore-mentioned Columb, surnamed

Coilrigin, was dying in a good old age, even at that very moment when he departed from the body St. Columba, who was then in Iona, thus addressed a few of the senior brethren who were standing around him, "Columb Coilrigin, the blacksmith, has not labored in vain, seeing that he has had the happiness, as he desired, to purchase the eternal rewards by the labor of his hands. For, behold, at this moment, his soul is carried by the holy angels to the joys of the heavenly country, because he laid out all that he could earn by his trade in alms to the poor."

Chapter 11
Of a Similar Vision of Angels

In like manner, on another occasion, whilst the holy man was living in the island of Iona, he one day suddenly raised his eyes to heaven and uttered the words, "O happy woman! Happy because of thy virtues; the angels of God are now carrying thy soul to paradise." Now these words from the mouth of the saint were heard by a certain religious brother, a Saxon, by name Genere, who was at the moment working at his trade, which was that of a baker. And on the same day of the month, at the end of the same year, the saint addressed the same Genere the Saxon, and said, "I see a wonderful thing; behold, the woman of whom I spoke in your presence last year, now meets in the air the soul of her husband, a poor and holy man, and together with the holy angels engage in a contest for it against the adverse powers; by their united assistance, and by the aid of the virtuous character of the man himself, his soul is rescued from the assaults of the demons, and brought to the place of eternal refreshment."

Chapter 12
Of the Holy Angels Whom Saint Columba Beheld Meeting in its Passage the Soul of Saint Brenden, the Founder of the Monastery Which in Scotic is Called Birra (Birr, in King's County)

On another day also, while the venerable man was residing on Iona, he called very early in the morning for his attendant, Diormit, so frequently mentioned before, and commanded him saying, "Make ready in haste for the celebration of the Holy Eucharist, for today is the birthday of blessed Brenden."

"Wherefore," said his attendant, "do you order such solemnities of the Mass to be prepared today? For no messenger hath come to us from Scotia (Ireland) to tell us of the death of that holy man."

"Go," said the saint, "it is thy duty to obey my commands. For this last night I saw the heavens suddenly open, and choirs of angels descend to meet the soul of the holy Brenden; and so great and incomparable was the brightness, that in that same hour it illuminated the whole world."

Chapter 13
Of the Holy Angels Who Carried off to Heaven the Soul of the Bishop, Saint Columban Mocu Loigse

On another day also, while the brethren were putting on their sandals in the morning, and were making ready to go to their different duties in the monastery, the saint, on the contrary, bade them rest that day and prepare for the holy sacrifice, ordering also some addition to be made to their dinner, as on the Lord's day. "I must," said he, "though unworthy, celebrate today the holy mysteries of the Eucharist, out of veneration to that soul which this last night went up to paradise, beyond the region of the stars in the heavens, borne thither amid the holy choirs of the angels."

At these words the brethren obeyed, and, according to his directions, rested that day; then, after preparing for the due celebration of the sacred rite, they accompanied the saint to the church in their white robes as on a festival. But it came to pass that when in the course of chanting the offices, the prayer was being sung as usual in which St. Martin's name is commemorated, the saint, suddenly turning to the chanters, when they had come to make mention of that name, said, "You must pray today for St. Columban, bishop." Then all the brethren present understood that Columban, a bishop in Leinster, the dear friend of Columba, had passed to the Lord. A short time after, some persons, who came from the province of Leinster, told how the bishop died in the very night in which it was thus made known to the saint.⁶

Chapter 14
Of the Apparition of Angels Who Had Come Down to Meet the Souls of the Monks of Saint Comgell

At another time, when the venerable man was living in island of Iona, he became suddenly excited, and summoned the brethren together by the sound of the bell. "Now," said he, "let us help by our prayers the monks of the Abbot Comgell, who are just now in danger of being drowned in the Lake of the Calf (Belfast Lough); for, lo! At this moment they are fighting against the hostile powers in the air, and are striving to rescue the soul of some stranger who is also drowning along with them." Then after having wept and prayed fervently, he hastily stood erect before the altar with a joyful countenance, whilst the brethren continued to lie prostrate in prayer. "Give thanks," he said, "to Christ, for now the holy angels, coming to the aid of holy souls, have rescued this stranger from the attacks of the demons, and borne him off in triumph like victorious warriors."

Chapter 15
*Of the Vision of the Angels Who Came to Meet
the Soul of One Emchath*

At another time, when the saint was travelling beyond the Dorsal
Ridge of Britain (Drumalban), near the lake of the River Nesa
(Loch Ness), he was suddenly inspired by the Holy Ghost, and said
to the brethren that accompanied him, "Let us go quickly to meet
the holy angels, who have been sent from the realms of the highest
heaven to carry away with them the soul of a heathen, and now
wait our arrival there, that we may baptize in due time before his
death this man, who has preserved his natural goodness through
all his life, even to extreme old age." And having said this much,
the holy old man hurried his companions as much as he could, and
walked before them until he came to a district called Airchart-dan
(Arochdan, now Glen Urquhart); and there he found an aged man
whose name was Emchat, who, on hearing the word of God
preached by the saint, believed and was baptized, and immediately
after, full of joy, and safe from evil, and accompanied by the
angels, who came to meet him, passed to the Lord. His son Virolec
also believed, and was baptized with all his house.

Chapter 16
*Of the Angel of the Lord That Came to the Relief of
the Brother who fell From the top of the Round Monastery
in the Oakwood Plain*

At another time, while the holy man sat in his little cell engaged
in writing, on a sudden his countenance changed, and he poured
forth this cry from his pure breast, saying, "Help! Help!" Two of
the brothers who stood at the door, namely, Colga, son of Cellach,
and Lugne Mocublai, asked the cause of such a sudden cry. The
venerable man answered, saying, "I ordered the angel of the Lord
who was just now standing among you to go quickly to the relief

of one of the brothers who is falling from the highest point of a large house which is now being built in the Oakwood Plain (Derry). And the saint added afterwards these words, saying, "How wonderful and almost unspeakable is the swiftness of angelic motion, like, as I imagine, to the rapidity of lightning. For the heavenly spirit who just now flew away from us when that man began to fall, arrived there to support him, as it were, in the twinkling of an eye, before his body reached the ground; nor was the man who fell able to feel any fracture or bruise. How wonderful, I say, is that most swift and timely help which could be given so very quickly, even though such an extent of land and sea lay between!"

Chapter 17
Of the Multitude of Holy Angels that Were Seen to Come Down
From Heaven at the Bidding of the Blessed Man

Another time also, while the blessed man was living in Iona, he made this known to the assembled brethren with very great earnestness, saying, "Today I wish to go alone to the western plain of this island; let none of you therefore follow me." They obeyed, and he went alone, as he desired.

But a brother, who was cunning, and of a prying disposition, proceeded by another road, and secretly placed himself on the summit of a certain little hill which overlooked the plain, because he was very anxious to learn the blessed man's motive for going out alone. While the spy on the top of the hill was looking upon him as he stood on a mound in the plain, with arms extended upwards, and eyes raised to heaven in prayer, then, strange to tell, behold a wonderful scene presented itself, which that brother, as I think not without the leave of God, witnessed with his own eyes from his place on the neighboring hill, that the saint's name and the reverence due to him might afterwards, even against his wishes, be more widely diffused among the people, through the vision thus vouchsafed. For holy angels, the citizens of the heavenly country, clad in white robes and flying with wonderful speed, began to stand around the saint whilst he prayed; and after a short converse with the blessed man, that heavenly host, as if feeling itself detected, flew speedily back again to the highest heavens. The blessed man himself also, after his meeting with the angels, returned to the monastery, and calling the brethren together a second time, asked, with no little chiding and reproof, which of them was guilty of violating his command. When all were declaring they did not know at all of the matter, the brother, conscious of his inexcusable transgression, and no longer able to conceal his guilt, fell on his knees before the saint in the midst of the assembled brethren, and humbly craved forgiveness. The saint, taking him aside, commanded him under heavy threats, as he knelt, never, during the life of the blessed man, to disclose to any person even the least part of the secret regarding the angels' visit. It was, therefore, after the saint's departure from the body that the brother related that manifestation of the heavenly host, and solemnly attested its truth. Whence, even to this day, the place where the angels assembled is called by a name that bears witness to the event that took place in it; this may be said to be in Latin "Colliculus Angelorum" and is in Scotic Cnoc Angel (now called Sithean Mor).[7] Hence, therefore, we must notice, and even carefully inquire, into the fact how great and of what kind these sweet visits of angels to this blessed man were, which took place mostly during the winter nights, when he was in watching and prayer in lonely places while others slept. These were no doubt very numerous, and could in no way come to the knowledge of other men. Though some of these which happened by night or by day might perhaps be discovered by one means or another, these must have been very few compared with the angelic visions, which, of course, could be known by nobody. The same observation applies in the same way to other bright apparitions hitherto investigated by few, which shall be afterwards described.

Chapter 18
Of the Bright Pillar Seen to Glow Upon the Saint's Head

Another time four holy founders of monasteries came from Scotia (Ireland), to visit St. Columba, and found him in the Hinba island (Eilean-na-Naoimh). The names of these distinguished men were Comgell Mocu Aridi, Cainnech Mocu Dalon, Brenden Mocu Alti, and Cormac, grandson of Leathain. They all with one consent agreed that St. Columba should consecrate, in their presence in the church, the holy mysteries of the Eucharist. The saint complied with their express desire, and entered the church with them on Sunday as usual, after the reading of the Gospel; and there, during the celebration of the solemn offices of the Mass, St. Brenden Mocu Alti saw, as he told Comgell and Cainnech afterwards, a ball of fire like a comet burning very brightly on the head of Columba, while he was standing before the altar, and consecrating the holy oblation, and thus it continued burning and rising upwards like a column, so long as he continued to be engaged in the same most sacred mysteries.

Chapter 19
Of the Visit of the Holy Ghost

At another time, when the saint was living in the Hinba island (Eilean-na-Naoimh), the grace of the Holy Ghost was communicated to him abundantly and unspeakably, and dwelt with him in a wonderful manner, so that for three whole days, and as many nights, without either eating or drinking, he allowed no one to approach him, and remained confined in a house which was filled with heavenly brightness. Yet out of that house, through the chinks of the doors and keyholes, rays of surpassing brilliancy were seen to issue during the night. Certain spiritual songs also, which had never been heard before, he was heard to sing. He came to see, as he allowed in the presence of a very few afterwards, many secrets hidden from men since the beginning of the world fully revealed; certain very obscure and difficult parts of sacred Scripture also were made quite plain, and clearer than the light to the eye of his pure heart. He grieved that his beloved disciple, Baithen, was not with him, because if he had chanced to be beside him during those three days, he would have been able to explain from the lips of the blessed man mysteries regarding past or future ages, unknown to the rest of mankind, and to interpret also some passages of the Sacred Volumes. However, Baithen was then detained by contrary winds in the Egean island (Egg), and he was not, therefore, able to be present until those three days and as many nights of that glorious and unspeakable visitation came to a close.

Chapter 20
Of Virgnous and the Angelic Splendor of light[8]

One winter's night the fore-mentioned Virgnous, burning with the love of God, entered the church alone to pray, while the others were asleep; and he prayed fervently in a little side chamber attached to the walls of the oratory. After a considerable interval, as it were of an hour, the venerable Columba entered the same sacred house, and along with him, at the same time, a golden light, that came down from the highest heavens and filled that part of the church. Even the separate recess of the side-chamber, where Virgnous was striving to hide himself as much as he could, was also filled, to his great alarm, with some of the brilliance of that heavenly light which burst through the inner-door of the chamber, that was a little open. And as no one can look directly at, or gaze with steady eye on, the summer sun in his mid-day splendor, so Virgnous could not at all bear this heavenly brightness which he saw, because of the brilliant and unspeakable radiance which overpowered his sight. The brother spoken of was so much terrified by the splendor, almost as dreadful as lightning that no strength remained in him. But, after a short prayer, St. Columba left the church.

The next day he sent for Virgnous, who was very much alarmed, and spoke to him these few consoling words: "You are crying to good purpose, my child, for last night you wert very pleasing in the sight of God by keeping thine eyes fixed on the ground when you were overwhelmed with fear at the brightness, for had you not done so, that priceless light would have blinded thine eyes. This, however, you must carefully observe: never to disclose this great manifestation of light while I live."

This circumstance, therefore, which is so wonderful and so worthy of record, became known to many after the saint's death through this same Virgnous's relating it. Comman, sister's son to Virgnous, a respected priest, solemnly assured me, Adomnán, of the truth of the vision I have just described, and he added, moreover, that he heard the story from the lips of the abbot Virgnous, his own uncle, who, as far as he could, had seen that vision.

Chapter 21
Of Another Very Similar Vision of Great Brilliance

Another night also, one of the brothers, whose name was Colga, the son of Aid Draigniche, of the grandsons of Fechrech mentioned in the first book,[9] came by chance, while the other brothers were asleep, to the gate of the church, and stood there for some time praying. Then suddenly he saw the whole church filled with a heavenly light, which more quickly than he could tell, flashed like lightning from his gaze. He did not know that St. Columba was praying at that time in the church, and after this sudden appearance of light, he returned home in great alarm.

On the following day the saint called him aside and rebuked him severely, saying: "Take care of one thing, my child, that you do not attempt to spy out and pry too closely into the nature of that heavenly light which was not granted you, but rather fled from you, and that you do not tell anyone during my lifetime what you have seen."

Chapter 22
Of Another Like Apparition of Divine Light

At another time also, the blessed man gave strict orders one day to Berchan, surnamed Mesloen, a pupil learning wisdom with them, saying "Take care, my son, that you come not near my little hut this evening, as you are always accustomed to do."

Berchan however, though hearing this, went, contrary to this command, to the blessed man's house in the dead of night while others were at rest, and cunningly put down his eyes on a line with the keyholes, in the hope that, just as the thing happened, some heavenly vision would be shown to the saint within. And at that very time the little hut was filled with a light of heavenly brightness, which the disobedient young man was not able to look upon, and therefore he fled at once from the spot.

On the morrow the saint took him apart, and chiding him severely, addressed him in these words: "Last night, my son, you sinned before God, and you did vainly imagine that the prying of your secret inquisitiveness could be hidden or concealed from the Holy Ghost. Did I not see you at that hour as you drew near to the door of my hut, and as you did go away from it? Had I not prayed for you at that moment, you would have fallen dead there before the door, or your eyes would have been torn out of their sockets; but on my account, the Lord has spared you at this time. And be assured of this also, that, whilst you are living in luxury in your own country of Hibernia, your face shall burn with shame all the days of your life. Yet by my prayers, I have obtained this favor of

God, that, as you are my disciple, you shall do heartfelt penance before death, and thus obtain the mercy of God." All these things, according to the saying of the blessed man, occurred afterwards to him as had been foretold regarding him.

Chapter 23
Of the Angels Whom the Saint saw Coming to Meet his Soul, as if to Show That it was About to Leave the Body

At another time, while the blessed man was living in the island of Iona, his holy countenance one day was lighted up suddenly with strange transports of joy; and raising his eyes to heaven he was filled with delight, and rejoiced beyond measure. After an interval of a few seconds, that sweet and enchanting delight was changed into a mournful sadness.

Now, the two men, who at the same hour were standing at the door of his hut, which was built on the higher ground, and were themselves also much afflicted with him (of whom the one was Lugne Mocublai, and the other a Saxon named Pilu) asked the cause of this sudden joy, and of the sorrow which followed. The saint said to them, "Go in peace, and do not ask me now to explain the cause of either that joy or that sadness."

On hearing this they humbly asked him, kneeling before him in tears, and with faces sunk to the ground, to grant their desire of knowing something concerning that matter which at that same hour had been revealed to the saint. Seeing them so much afflicted, he said, "On account of my love to you, I do not wish you to be in sadness; but you must first promise me never to disclose to any one during my life the secret you seek to know." They made of course the promise at once according to his request, and then, when the promise was made, the venerable man spoke to them thus: "On this very day, thirty years of my sojourn in Britain have been completed, and meanwhile for many days past I have been devoutly asking of my Lord to release me from my dwelling here at the end of this thirtieth year, and to call me thither to my heavenly fatherland. And this was the cause of that joy of mine, of which in sorrowful mood you ask me. For I saw the holy angels sent down from the lofty throne to meet my soul when it is taken from the flesh. But, behold now how they are stopped suddenly, and stand on a rock at the other side of the sound of our island, evidently being anxious to come near me and deliver me from the body. But they are not allowed to come nearer, because, that thing which God granted me after praying with my whole strength— namely, that I might pass from the world to Him on this day—He has changed in a moment in His listening to the prayers of so many churches for me. These churches have no doubt prayed as the Lord has granted, so that, though it is against my ardent wish, four years from this day are added for me to abide in the flesh. Such a sad delay as this was fitly the cause of the grief today. At the end of these four years, then, which by God's favor my life is yet to see, I shall pass away suddenly, without any previous bodily sickness, and depart with joy to the Lord, accompanied by His holy angels, who shall come to meet me at that hour."

According to these words, which the venerable man uttered, it is said, with much sorrow and grief, and even many tears, he afterwards abode in the flesh for four years.

Chapter 24
How our Patron, Saint Columba, Passed to the Lord

Towards the end of the above-mentioned four years, and as a true prophet he knew long before that his death would follow the close of that period, the old man, worn out with age, went in a cart one day in the month of May, as we mentioned in the preceding second book, to visit some of the brethren who were at work. And having found them at work on the western side of Iona, he began to speak to them that day, saying, "During the paschal solemnities in the month of April now past, with desire have I desired to depart to Christ the Lord, as He had allowed me, if I preferred it. But lest a joyous festival should be turned for you into mourning, I thought it better to put off for a little longer the time of my departure from the world." The beloved monks all the while they were hearing this sad news were greatly addicted, and he endeavored as well as he could to cheer them with words of consolation. Then, having done this, he turned his face to the east, still seated as he was in his chariot, and blessed the island with its inhabitants; and from that day to the present, as we have stated in the book above mentioned, the venomous reptiles with the three forked tongues could do no manner of harm to man or beast. After uttering these words of blessing, the saint was carried back to his monastery.

Then, again, a few days afterwards, while he was celebrating the solemn offices of the Mass as usual on the Lord's day, the face of the venerable man, as his eyes were raised to heaven, suddenly appeared as if suffused with a ruddy glow, for, as it is written, "A glad heart maketh a cheerful countenance."[10] For at that same hour he alone saw an angel of the Lord hovering above within the walls of his oratory; and as the lovely and tranquil aspect of the holy angels infuses joy and exultation into the hearts of the elect, this was the cause of that sudden joy infused into the blessed man.

When those who were present on the occasion inquired as to the cause of that joy with which he was evidently inspired, the saint looking upwards gave them this reply, "Wonderful and unspeakable is the subtility of the angelic nature! For lo, an angel of the Lord, who was sent to demand a certain deposit dear to God, has, after looking down upon us within the church, and blessing us, returned again through the roof of the church, without leaving any trace of his passage out." Thus spoke the saint.

But none of the bystanders could understand what kind of a deposit the angel was sent to demand. Our patron, however, gave the name of a holy deposit to his own soul that had been entrusted to him by God; and after an interval of six days from that time, as shall be related further on, he departed to the Lord on the night of the Lord's day. In the end, then, of this same week, that is on the day of the Sabbath, the venerable man, and his pious attendant Diormit, went to bless the barn which was near at hand. When the saint had entered in and blessed it, and the two heaps of winnowed corn that were in it, he gave expression to his thanks in these words, saying, "I heartily congratulate my beloved monks, that this year also, if I am obliged to depart from you, you will have a sufficient supply for the year."

On hearing this, Diormit his attendant began to feel sad, and said, "This year, at this time, father, you very often vex us, by so frequently making mention of your leaving us."

But the saint replied to him, "I have a little secret address to make to you, and if you will promise me faithfully not to reveal it to any one before my death, I shall be able to speak to you with more freedom about my departure." When his attendant had on bended knees made the promise as the saint desired, the venerable man thus resumed his address: "This day in the Holy Scriptures is called the Sabbath, which means rest. And this day is indeed a Sabbath to me, for it is the last day of my present laborious life, and on it I rest after the fatigues of my labors; and this night at midnight, which commences the solemn Lord's Day, I shall, according to the sayings of Scripture, go the way of our fathers. For already my Lord Jesus Christ deigns to invite me; and to Him, I say, in the middle of this night shall I depart, at His invitation. For so it has been revealed to me by the Lord himself." The attendant hearing these sad words began to weep bitterly, and the saint endeavored to console him as well as he could.

After this the saint left the barn, and in going back to the monastery, rested half way at a place where a cross, which was afterwards erected, and is standing to this day, fixed into a millstone, may be observed on the roadside. While the saint, as I have said, bowed down with old age, sat there to rest a little, behold, there came up to him a white pack-horse, the same that used, as a willing servant, to carry the milk-vessels from the cowshed to the monastery. It came up to the saint and, strange to say, laid its head on his bosom-inspired, I believe, by God to do so, as each animal is gifted with the knowledge of things according to the will of the Creator; and knowing that its master was soon about to leave it, and that it would see him no more, began to utter plaintive cries, and like a human being, to shed copious tears on the saint's bosom, foaming and greatly wailing. The attendant, seeing this, began to drive the weeping mourner away, but the saint forbade him, saying: "Let it alone, as it is so fond of me, let it pour out its bitter grief into my bosom. Lo! You are a man, and as you have a rational soul, can know nothing of my departure hence, except what I myself have just told you, but to this brute beast devoid of reason, the Creator Himself has evidently in some way made it known that its master is going to leave it." And saying this, the saint blessed the work-horse, which turned away from him in sadness.

Then leaving this spot, he ascended the hill that overlooks the monastery, and stood for some little time on its summit; and as he stood there with both hands uplifted, he blessed his monastery, saying, "Small and mean though this place is, yet it shall be held in great and unusual honor, not only by Scotic kings and people, but also by the rulers of foreign and barbarous nations, and by their subjects; the saints also even of other churches shall regard it with no common reverence."

After these words he descended the hill, and having returned to the monastery sat in his hut transcribing the Psalter, and coming to that verse of the 33rd Psalm[11] where it is written, "They that seek the Lord shall want no manner of thing that is good," "Here," said he, "at the end of the page, I must stop; and what follows let Baithene write." The last verse he had written was very applicable to the saint, who was about to depart, and to whom eternal goods shall never be wanting; while the one that follows is equally applicable to the father who succeeded him, the instructor of his spiritual children: "Come, ye children, and hearken unto me: I will teach you the fear of the Lord;" and indeed he succeeded him, as recommended by him, not only in teaching, but also in writing.

Having written the aforementioned verse at the end of the page, the saint went to the church to the nocturnal vigils of the Lord's Day; and so soon as this was over, he returned to his chamber, and spent the remainder of the night on his bed, where he had a bare flagstone for his couch, and for his pillow a stone, which stands to this day as a kind of monument beside his grave. While then he was reclining there, he gave his last instructions to the brethren, in the hearing of his attendant alone, saying: "These, O my children, are the last words I address to you: That ye be at peace, and have unfeigned charity among yourselves; and if you thus follow the example of the holy fathers, God, the Comforter of the good, will be your Helper and I, abiding with Him, will intercede for you; and He will not only give you sufficient to supply the wants of this present life, but will also bestow on you the good and eternal rewards which are laid up for those that keep His commandments." Thus far have the last words of our venerable patron, as he was about to leave this weary pilgrimage for his heavenly country, been preserved for recital in our brief narrative.

After these words, as the happy hour of his departure gradually approached, the saint became silent. Then as soon as the bell tolled at midnight, he rose hastily, and went to the church; and running more quickly than the rest, he entered it alone, and knelt down in prayer beside the altar. At the same moment his attendant Diormit, who more slowly followed him, saw from a distance that the whole interior of the church was filled with a heavenly light in the direction of the saint. And as he drew near to the door, the same light he had seen, and which was also seen by a few more of the brethren standing at a distance, quickly disappeared. Diormit therefore entering the church, cried out in a mournful voice, "Where are you, father?" And feeling his way in the darkness, as the brethren had not yet brought in the lights, he found the saint lying before the altar; and raising him up a little, he sat down beside him, and laid his holy head on his bosom. Meanwhile the rest of the monks ran in hastily in a body with their lights, and beholding their dying father, burst into lamentations. And the saint, as we have been told by some who were present, even before his soul departed, opened wide his eyes and looked round him from side to side, with a countenance full of wonderful joy and gladness, no doubt seeing the holy angels coming to meet him. Diormit then raised the holy right hand of the saint, that he might bless his assembled monks. And the venerable father himself moved his hand at the same time, as well as he was able, that as he could not in words, while his soul was departing, he might at least, by the motion of his hand, be seen to bless his brethren. And having given them his holy benediction in this way, he immediately breathed his last.

After his soul had left the tabernacle of the body, his face still continued ruddy, and brightened in a wonderful way by his vision of the angels, and that to such a degree that he had the appearance, not so much of one dead, as of one alive and sleeping. Meanwhile the whole church resounded with loud lamentations of grief.

I must not omit to mention the revelation made to a certain saint of Ireland, at the very time the blessed soul departed. For in that monastery which in the Scotic language is called Clonifinchoil (now Rosnarea, in parish of Knockcommon, Meath), there was a holy man named Lugud, son of Tailchan, one who had grown old in the service of Christ, and was noted for his sanctity and wisdom. Now this man had a vision which at early dawn he told in great affliction to one called Fergnous, who was like himself a servant of Christ. "In the middle of this last night," said he, "Columba, the pillar of many churches, passed to the Lord; and at the moment of his blessed departure, I saw in the spirit the whole Ionan island, where I never was in the body, resplendent with the brightness of angels; and the whole heavens above it, up to the very zenith, were illumined with the brilliant light of the same heavenly messengers, who descended in countless numbers to bear away his holy soul. At the same moment, also, I heard the loud hymns and entrancingly sweet canticles of the angelic host, as his holy soul was borne aloft amidst the ascending choirs of angels." Virgnous, who about this time came over from Ireland, and spent the rest of his life in the Hinba island (Eilean-na-Naoimh), very often related to the monks of St. Columba this vision of angels, which, as has been said, he undoubtedly heard from the lips of the old man himself, to whom it had been granted. This same Virgnous, having for many years lived without reproach in obedience amongst the brethren, led the life of an anchorite, as a victorious soldier of Christ, for twelve years more, in the hermitage of Muirbulcmar. This vision above mentioned we have not only found in writing, but have heard related with the utmost freedom by several well-informed old men to whom Virgnous himself had told it.

Another vision also given at the same hour under a different form was related to me, Adomnán, who was a young man at the time, by one of those who had seen it; and who solemnly assured me of its truth. He was a very old man, a servant of Christ, whose name may be called Ferreol, but in the Scotic tongue Ernene, of the race of Mocufirroide, who, as being himself a holy monk, is buried in the Ridge of Tomma (now Drumhome, county Donegal), amidst the remains of other monks of St. Columba, and awaits the resurrection with the saints; he said: "On that night when St. Columba, by a happy and blessed death, passed from earth to heaven, while I and others with me were engaged in fishing in the valley of the river Fend (the Finn, in Donegal), which abounds in fish, we saw the whole vault of heaven become suddenly illuminated. Struck by the suddenness of the miracle, we raised our eyes and looked towards the east, when, lo! There appeared something like an immense pillar of fire, which seemed to us, as it ascended upwards at that midnight, to illuminate the whole earth like the summer sun at noon; and after that column penetrated the heavens darkness followed, as if the sun had just set. And not only did we, who were together in the same place, observe with intense surprise the brightness of this remarkable luminous pillar, but many other fishermen also, who were engaged in fishing here and there in different deep pools along the same river, were greatly terrified, as they afterwards related to us, by an appearance of the same kind." These three miraculous visions, then, which were seen at the very hour of our venerable patron's departure, show clearly that the Lord hath conferred on him eternal honors. But let us now return to our narrative.

After his holy soul had departed, and the matin hymns were finished, his sacred body was carried by the brethren, chanting psalms, from the church back to his chamber, from which a little before he had come alive; and his obsequies were celebrated with all due honor and reverence for three days and as many nights. And when these sweet praises of God were ended, the venerable body of our holy and blessed patron was wrapped in a clean shroud of fine linen, and, being placed in the coffin prepared for it, was buried with all due veneration, to rise again with lustrous and eternal brightness.

And now, near the close of this book, we shall relate what has been told us by persons cognizant of the facts, regarding the above-mentioned three days during which his obsequies were celebrated in due ecclesiastical form. It happened on one occasion that a certain brother speaking with great simplicity in the presence of the holy and venerable man, said to him, "After your death all the people of these provinces will row across to Iona to celebrate your obsequies, and will entirely fill it."

Hearing this said the saint immediately replied: "No, my child, the event will not turn out as you say; for a promiscuous throng of people shall not by any means be able to come to my obsequies: none but the monks of my monastery will perform my funeral rites, and grace the last offices bestowed upon me." And the fulfillment of this prophecy was brought about immediately after his death by God's almighty power, for there arose a storm of wind without rain, which blew so violently during those three days and nights of his obsequies, that it entirely prevented everyone from crossing the sound in his little boat. And immediately after the interment of the blessed man, the storm was quelled at once, the wind ceased, and the, whole sea became calm.

Let the reader therefore think in what and how great honor our illustrious patron was held by God, seeing that, while he was yet in this mortal flesh, God was pleased at his prayer to quell the storms and to calm the seas; and again, when he found it necessary, as on the occasion just mentioned, the gales of wind arose as he wished, and the sea was lashed into fury; and this storm, as hath been said, was immediately, so soon as his funeral rites were performed, changed into a great calm. Such, then, was the end of our illustrious patron's life, and such is an earnest of all his merits.

And now, according to the sentence of the Holy Scriptures, sharing in eternal triumphs, added to the patriarchs, associated with the prophets and apostles, numbered amongst the thousands of white-robed saints, who have washed their robes in the blood of the Lamb, he follows the Lamb whithersoever He goes; a virgin immaculate, free from all stain, through the grace of our Lord Jesus Christ: to whom, with the Father, be honor, and power, and praise, and glory, and eternal dominion, in the unity of the Holy Ghost for ever and ever.

After reading these three books, let the diligent reader observe of what and how great merit, of what and how high honor in the sight of God our holy and venerable abbot must have been deemed worthy, how great and many were the bright visits of the angels made to him, how full of the prophetic spirit, how great his power of miracles wrought in God, how often and to what great extent, while yet he was abiding in this mortal flesh, he was surrounded by a halo of heavenly light; and how, even after the departure of his most kindly soul from the tabernacle of the body, until the present day the place where his sacred bones repose, as has been clearly shown to certain chosen persons, doth not cease to be frequently visited by the holy angels, and illumined by the same heavenly brightness. And this unusual favor hath been conferred by God on this same man of blessed memory; that though he lived in this small and remote island of the British sea, his name has not only become illustrious throughout the whole of our own Ireland, and Britain, the largest island of the whole world, but hath reached even unto triangular Spain, and into Gaul, and to Italy, which lies beyond the Penine Alps; and also to the city of Rome itself, the head of all cities. This great and honorable celebrity, amongst other marks of divine favor, is known to have been conferred on this same saint by God, Who loves those that love Him, and raises them to immense honor by glorifying more and more those that magnify and truly praise Him, Who is blessed for evermore. Amen.

I beseech those who wish to transcribe these books, yea, rather I adjure them by Christ, the Judge of the world, after they have diligently transcribed, carefully to compare and correct their copies with that from which they have copied them, and also to subjoin here this adjuration:

Whoever reads these books on the virtues of St. Columba, let him pray to the Lord for me, Dorbbene, that after death I may possess eternal life.

Book Three Notes

1 The excommunication may have followed the famous Battle of Cúl Dreimhne , the "Battle of the Book", which took place in 561 over a dispute with St. Finnian over St. Columba's right to keep a psalter which he had copied. The quarrel became a pitched battle fought between King Diarmait mac Cerbaill and the Uí Néill clan which resulted in 3,000 deaths.

2 St. Brendan of Birr, or "Brendan the Elder", not to be confused with St. Brendan the Navigator, who also a contemporary.

3 Finnio is an affectionate name for St. Findbarr.

4 Aidan was *King* of Dál Riata from 574-609.

5 The battle of Magh Rath, fought 637.

6 Not the more famous St. Columban, Abbot of Bobbio in Italy. Possibly the Columban mentioned in Book II.14.

7 The location of Sithean Mor is still known to this day, the spot being marked by a little cairn. Over the ages, the locals have identified the angels of St. Adomnán with fairies. The location is called "Fairy Hill" and is the subject of all sorts of superstitions.

8 Adomnán's original title for this chapter is "Of the angelic splendor of the light which Virgnous-a youth of good disposition, and afterwards made by God superior of this Church in which I, though unworthy, now serve-saw coming down upon St. Columba in the Church, on a winter's night, when the brethren were at rest in their chambers."

9 Book I.35

10 Prov. 15:13

11 Psalm 34 in the modern numeration.

Appendix
Hymns of Saint Columba

Besides his renown as a saint, evangelist, and missionary, St. Columba had a reputation in his own day as a talented scribe and poet. Recall that St. Columba's condemnation in the affair of the Battle of Cúl Dreimhne originated in a dispute about his right to copy St. Finnian's Psalter. St. Adomnán tells us in Book Two, Chapter 8 of "a volume written by the sacred fingers of St. Columba"; later in the same place he mentions "a book of hymns for the office of every day in the week...in the handwriting of St. Columba." Our saint seems to have had a special love for writing and illuminating manuscripts that stayed with him throughout his tumultuous life.

We can only hypothesize on the contents of the books mentioned by St. Adomnán. Did the "book of hymns" written by Columba include his own compositions? We have no way of knowing, but Irish tradition has been constant in attributing several hymns to St. Columba. Others are probably not by Columba but are nonetheless closely connected with the age of early Celtic missionary activity at Iona. We include in this appendix both those that have been attributed to Columba as well as those linked to Iona during its golden age prior to the Viking invasions.

Of all the texts in the corpus of St. Columba, the *Altus Prosator* holds pride of place. It is universal and even apocalyptic in scope, spanning twenty-three stanzas from the Creation to the Last Judgment. Its sober refrain on the despising of worldly pleasures denotes a liturgical use for this hymn, though we do not know exactly in what setting the song was used. Its length suggests some sort of sequence for an important feast day, akin to the *Vexilla Regis* or the *Dies Irae*, although this is pure conjecture. The attribution of the *Altus Prosator* to St. Columba dates only to the 11th century, where it is found in the prefaces of the two copies of the Irish *Liber hymnorum*, so like all other writings attributed to Columba, one must be cautious in affirming too much. The English translation we feature here was translated by Church of Scotland minister Duncan MacGregor of Inveralocchy (1854-1923), a famous historian of early Scottish Christianity.

Let Christian Men, arranged by Rev. W. McClelland, is of uncertain origin. It has been attributed to the monks of Iona and was originally in Latin, but the author has been unable to track down the original Latin or any use of this hymn that predates the late 19th century.

The hymn *Christ the World's Redeemer* is better known by the Latin title *Christus Redemptor Omnium*. It was translated by Duncan MacGregor and arranged by Anglican composer John Farmer (d. 1901). It is a simple yet powerful hymn of praise to Christ and the glory of the martyrs, invoking the aid of Jesus as armor and seeking triumph through his cross. It has unfortunately been overshadowed by the much more well-known hymn *Christus Redemptor Omnium*, a Gregorian melody of the 6th century sung at Vespers for Christmas as popularized by Pope Urban VIII's 1629 breviary. We have also included the Latin of *Christus Redemptor Omnium*, found in *Latin Hymns* by Matthew Germing S.J., Loyola University Press, 1920.

The hymn *Alone with None but Thee, My God* comes from an ancient prayer called "Columba's Affirmation," which is a sort of rousing call to spiritual combat similar to St. Patrick's Breastplate. It was first set to music to the German tune *Auch Jetzt Macht* in the 1816 *Choralbuch* and was not translated into English until 1971 with its inclusion into the Anglican *Hymnbook*.

In Te Christe Credentium is one of the hymns most certainly attributable to Columba. It is related to *Christus Redemptor Omnium* and *Alone with None but Thee My God*, it's Latin perhaps providing the source material for the other two. Because of its similarity to *Christus Redemptor Omnium*, we have not included the Latin here.

The *Noli Pater* has also been attributed from the earliest days to St. Columba. A medieval legend suggests that the hymn was composed to check the progress of a fire, since it petitions to be delivered from the "shattering fear and fire." Others have suggested a connection with Midsummer's Eve fires and the Feast of St. John the Baptist, who is invoked at the end of the hymn, although others point out that the custom of the Midsummer bonfires did not exist in the pre-Danish Celtic Church. Others—such as the gloss on the 1898 Irish *Liber hymnorum* by John Henry Bernard—hypothesizes *Noli Pater* as a penitential hymn said specifically as a prayer against pestilence, such as that mentioned in Book Two, Chapters 4 and 47. We have included the English and Latin texts as found in the 1898 *Liber hymnorum*.

Finally there is the charming *Iona Boat Song*. The *Iona Boat Song* is often confused with the *Boat Song of Columbanus*, the latter being a rousing hymn of the Irish missionaries as they traveled the rivers of Europe founding monasteries. The *Iona Boat Song*, however, is a burial song. From the year 900 until the late 13th century, Iona was the final resting place of the Kings of Scotland, and the *Iona Boat Song* was chanted as their dead kings were ferried to Iona from the mainland for burial. Iona thus becomes a type of heaven, where the king finally finds rest from his labors, as suggested by the beautiful closing lines, "We are faring out West / To the dear isle Iona, my home / To the dear isle Iona, my home."

Part of the confusion in discerning which hymns can be ascribed to Columba's hand is related to the popular hymn tune "St. Columba." A hymn tune is simply a melody to which a hymn text is sung. Hymn tunes may be used with various different texts. An example of a hymn tune is the Kingsfold tune, which is used in *I Heard the Voice of Jesus Say* but also *O Sing a Song of Bethlehem*, in addition to multiple other texts. The St. Columba tune is probably most known from the hymn *The King of Love My Shepherd Is* but is also used in at least 20 other hymn texts. That there are so many hymns which have St. Columba as their tune designation has perhaps led to the error that these hymns actually date back to St. Columba or are related to ancient Iona.

Regardless of whether St. Columba's hand penned any of these hymns, they certainly help us enter into the heart of Columba's Iona and the evangelistic spirit of the age of the great Irish missions.

Altus Prosator

The High Creator, the Unbegotten of days,
was without origin of beginning, limitless.
He is and He will be for endless age of ages,
with whom is the only-begotten Christ,
and the Holy Spirit, co-eternal in the everlasting glory, but say
one God, saving our faith in three most glorious Persons.

*

He created good angels and archangels, the orders
of principalities and Thrones, of Power and of Virtues, so
that the goodness and majesty of the Trinity might not be
unproductive in all works of bounty, but might have
heavenly beings in which He might greatly show forth his
favors by a word of power.

*

From the summit of the Kingdom of Heavens, where angels
stand, from his radiant brightness, from the loveliness of his
own form,
through being proud Lucifer had fallen,
whom He had formed, and the apostate angels also, by the
same sad fall
of the author of vainglory and obstinate envy,
the rest continuing in their dominions.

*

The great Dragon, most loathsome, terrible and ancient,
which was the slippery serpent, more cunning than all beasts
and than all the fiercer living things of the earth,
dragged down with him a third of the stars to the pit of
infernal places and sundry prisons,
fugitives from the true light, hurled down by the Parasite.

*

The Most High, planning the frame and harmony of the
world, had made heaven and earth, had fashioned the sea and
the waters,
and also shoots of grass, the little trees of the woods, the sun,
the moon and the stars, fire and necessary things, birds, fish
and cattle, beasts and living creatures, and finally the first-
formed man, to rule with prophecy.

*

At once, when the stars were made, lights of the firmament,
the angels praised for His wonderful creating the Lord of this
immense mass,
the Craftsman of the heavens.

With a praiseworthy proclamation, fitting and unchanging, in an excellent symphony they gave thanks to the Lord, not by any endowment of nature, but out of love and choice.

*

Our first two parents having been assailed and led astray, the devil falls a second time, together with his retinue, by the horror of whose faces and the sound of whose flying frail men might be dismayed, stricken with fear,
unable to gaze with their bodily eyes on those
who are now bound in bundles in the bonds of their prisons.

*

Driven out of the midst, he was thrust down by the Lord;
the space of air is choked by a wild mass
of his treacherous attendants, invisible
lest, tainted by their wicked examples and their crimes—no fences or walls ever concealing them—
folk should sin openly, before the eyes of all.

*

Clouds bear wintry floods from the fountains of the Ocean, from the three deeper floods of the sea, to the expanse of the sky, in azure whirlwinds, to do good to the cornfields, the vines and the shoots; driven by the winds emerging from their treasuries
which dry up the corresponding sea-marshes.

*

The momentary glory of the kings of the present world, fleeting and tyrannical,
is cast down at God's whim.
See, giants are shown to groan in great affliction beneath the waters, to be scorched by fire and in torment, and stifled by

~ 166 ~

the swelling whirlpools of Cocytus, covered with rocks, they
are destroyed by billows and sharp stones.

*

The Lord often sifts down the waters bound in the clouds,
lest they should all at once break out, their barriers broken,
from whose most plentiful streams, as if from breasts,
slowly flowing across the tracts of the earth,
freezing and warming at different times,
the rivers flow everywhere, never failing.

*

By the divine powers of the great God is hung
the globe of the earth, and the circle of the great deep placed
about it,
held up by the strong hand of almighty God,
with columns like bars supporting it,
promontories and rocks as their solid foundations,
fixed firm, as if on certain immovable bases.

*

It seems doubtful to no one that there is a hell down below
where there are held to be in darkness, worms and dreadful
animals; where there is sulphurous fire burning with
voracious flames; where there is the screaming men,
weeping and gnashing of teeth; where there is the groaning
of Gehenna, terrible and ancient;
where there is the horrible fiery burning of thirst and hunger.

*

Under the earth, as we read, we know there are inhabitants
whose knee bends in prayer to the Lord, but for whom it was
impossible to open the written book sealed with seven seals
according to the warnings of Christ,

which he himself had unsealed after he had risen as victor,
fulfilling the prophets' foreseeing of his Coming.

*

Paradise was planted from the beginning by the Lord,
as we read in the most noble opening of Genesis,
from whose fountain-spring four rivers flow,
in whose flowery midst is also the Tree of Life
whose leaves, bearing healing for the nations, do not fall;
whose delights are indescribable and abundant.

*

Who has climbed Sinai, the appointed mountain of the Lord?
Who has heard the immeasurable thunders sounding?
Who has heard the clamour of the mighty war-trumpet
echoing?
Who has also seen the lightning flashing all around? Who
has seen the flashes and thunderbolts and crashing rocks,
except Moses, the judge of the people of Israel?

*

The day of the Lord, most righteous King of Kings, is at
hand: a day of anger and vindication, of darkness and of cloud,
a day of wonderful mighty thunders, a day also of
distress,
of sorrow and sadness,
in which the love and desire of women will cease
and the striving of men and the desire of this world.

*

We shall stand trembling before the Lord's judgement seat,
and we shall render an account of all our deeds, seeing also
our crimes placed before our gaze, and the books of
conscience thrown open before us. We will break out into

most bitter weeping and sobbing, the possibility of
repentance being taken away.

*

At the blast of the First Archangel's wonderful trumpet, the
strongest vaults and tombs shall break open, the chill of the
men of the present world melting away, the bones gathering
to their joints from every place, their ethereal, souls meeting
them, returning once more to their own dwelling places.

*

Orion wanders from his turning point at the hinge of heaven—
the Pleiades being left behind, most splendid of the stars—
across the boundaries of the sea, of its unknown eastern rim.
Vesper, wheeling in its fixed circuits, returns by the its
former paths, rising after two years in the evening. These
things employed as types are understood figuratively.

*

When Christ, the most-high Lord, comes down from the
heavens, the brightest sign and standard of the Cross will
shine forth.
The two principal lights being obscured,
the stars will fall to earth like the fruit of a fig-tree, and the
face of the world will be like the fire of a furnace. Then
armies will hide in the caves of the mountains.

*

By the singing of hymns eagerly ringing out,
by thousands of angels rejoicing in holy dances,
and by the four living creatures full of eyes, with
the twenty-four joyful elders casting their
crowns under the feet of the Lamb of God, the Trinity is
praised in eternal three-fold exchanges.

*

The raging anger of fire will devour the adversaries who will
not believe that Christ came from God the Father.
But we shall surely fly off to meet him straight away, and
thus we shall be with him in several ranks of dignities
according to the eternal merits of our rewards,
to abide in glory from age to age.

*

[Response]
Who can please God in the last time,
the noble ordinances of truth being changed,
except the despisers of this present world?

Let Christian Men

Let Christian men his praise proclaim
Whom once the friendly wave
From Erin brought, with zeal aflame,
Our fathers' souls to save.

The warlike pagan eagles fled
Before the dove of peace,
And faith by isle and inlet spread
And found a rich increase.

Iona's hallowed shrine became
a beacon to the world;
a banner of the sacred Name,
for all the seas unfurled.

O thou of kings true-born a king,
Of Christ the herald-dove,

O hear thy grateful children sing
Their joy of thee, their love.

Columba, with the heavenly host,
Make thine the praise we bring
To Father, Son and Holy Ghost,
Till all the earth shall ring.

Christ the World's Redeemer

Christ is the world's Redeemer,
The lover of the pure,
The fount of heavenly wisdom,
Our trust and hope secure;
The armor of His soldiers,
The Lord of earth and sky;
Our health while we are living,
Our life when we shall die.

Christ hath our host surrounded
With clouds of martyrs bright,
Who wave their palms in triumph,
And fire us for the fight.
Christ the red cross ascended,
To save a world undone,
And, suffering for the sinful,
Our full redemption won.

All glory to the Father,
The unbegotten One;
All honor be to Jesus,
His sole begotten Son;
And to the Holy Spirit—

The perfect Trinity.
Let all the worlds give answer,
Amen—so let it be.

Christus Redemptor Omnium

Refrain:
Christus lorica militum.
Christus creator omnium.

Christus, redemptor gentium,
Christus, amator virginum,
Christus, fons sapientium,
Christus, fides credentium;

Christus, salus viventium
Et vita morientium,
Coronavit exercitum
Nostrum cum turba martyrum.

Christus crucem ascenderat,
Christus mundum salvaverat,
Christus et nos redemerat,
Christus pro nobis passus est;

Christus infernum penetrat,
Christus caelum ascenderat,
Christus cum Deo sederat,
Ubi nunquam defuerat.

Gloria haec altissimo
Deo Patri ingenito,
Honor ac summo Filio,
Unico, unigenito,

Spirituique optimo,
Sancto, perfecto, sedujo;
Amen, fiat perpetua
In sempiterna saecula.

Alone With None But Thee My God

Alone with none but thee, my God,
I journey on my way.
What need I fear when thou art near,
O King of night and day?
More safe am I within thy hand
than if a host should round me stand.

My destined time is known to thee,
and death will keep his hour;
did warriors strong around me throng,
they could not stay his power:
no walls of stone can man defend
when thou thy messenger dost send.

My life I yield to thy decree,
and bow to thy control
in peaceful calm, for from thine arm
no power can wrest my soul.
Could earthly omens e'er appal
a man that heeds the heavenly call?
The child of God can fear no ill,
his chosen dread no foe;
we leave our fate with thee, and wait
thy bidding when to go.
'Tis not from chance our comfort springs.
thou art our trust, O King of kings.

In Te Christe Credentium

Have mercy, Christ, have mercy
On all that trust in thee,
For thou art God in glory
To all eternity.

O God, make speed to save us
In life's abounding throes:
O God, make haste to help us
In all our weary woes.

O God, thou art the Father
Of all that have believed:
From whom all hosts of angels
Have life and power received.

Christ is the world's redeemer,
The lover of the pure,
The font of heavenly wisdom,
Our trust and hope secure.
The armor of his soldiers,
The Lord of earth and sky;
Our health while we are living,
Our life when we shall die.
Alone With None but Thee

Noli Pater

Father, do not allow thunder and lightning,
Lest we be shattered by its fear and fire.

We fear you, the terrible one, believing there is none like you.

All songs praise you throughout the host of angels.
Let the summits of heaven, too, praise you with roaming lightening,

O most loving Jesus, O righteous King of Kings.
Blessed forever, ruling in right government,

Is John before the Lord, till now in his mother's womb,
Filled with the grace of God in place of wine and strong drink.

Elizabeth of Zechariah begot a great man:
John the Baptist, the forerunner of the Lord.

The flame of the love of God remains in my heart as a gem placed in a silver vessel of gold.

Pater indulgere tonitrua cum fulgore ac frangamur formidine huius atque uridine

Te timemus terribilem nullum credentes similem te cuncta canunt carmina angelorum per agmina

Teque exultent culmina caeli uagi per fulmina O' Iesu amantissime o rex regum rectissime

Benedictus in ssecula recta regens regimina Iohannes coram domino adhuc matris in utero

Repletus dei gratia pro uino atque siccera Elizabeth et Zacharias uirum magnum genuit Iohannem baptizam precursorem domini

Manet in rneo corde dei amoris flamma ut in argenti vase auri ponitur gemma

Iona Boat Song

Softly glide we along,
Softly chant we our song
For a king who to resting is come.
O, beloved and best
We are faring out West
To the dear isle Iona, my home.

Calmly there shalt thou lie,
With thy fathers gone by,
Their dust mingled deep with thine own,
Ne'er again to awake,
Till the last dawn shall break
And the trump of the judgement is blown.

Softly glide we along,
Softly chant we our song,
For a king who to resting is come.
O beloved and best
We are faring out West,
To the dear isle Iona, my home
To the dear isle Iona, my home.

Prayer to Saint Columba[1]
(14th century Incholm)

Mouth of the dumb,
Light of the blind,
Foot of the lame,
To the fallen stretch out your hand.
Strengthen the senseless

Restore the mad
O Columba, hope of Scots,
By your merits' mediation.
Make us companions
of the blessed angels.

Appendix Notes

[1] From the "Inchcolm Antiphoner", Edinburgh University Library MS
211. Vi. Translated by Gilbert Márkus in Clancy, *The Triumph Tree*
(1998).

Made in United States
Troutdale, OR
01/27/2024

17213196R00106